SO-FIY-503

EMERGENCY IN PERSPECTIVE

The poor illiterate and semi-literate masses have for the first time made their voice felt on the issue of political liberty. And the credit mainly goes to them to have liberated a demoralised and disoriented elite that had abandoned the very ground which fostered its chief claim to the leadership of the nation.

EMERGENCY IN PERSPECTIVE

Reprieve and Challenge

Sachchidanand Sinha

Heritage Publishers
M-116, CONNAUGHT CIRCUS
NEW DELHI-110001

069651
40360

To

*The dumb millions who have brought
about our second liberation*

1977

© Sachohidanand Sinha

Published by B. R. Chawla for HERITAGE PUBLISHERS, M-116,
Connaught Circus, New Delhi-110001, and printed at
Dhawan Printing Works, A-26, Mayapuri, Phase-I,
New Delhi-110064

Contents

069651

40360

Preface

There have been many studies of the Emergency since the end of Mrs Gandhi's rule. But none of these studies have tried to come to grips with the basic issues involved. Once the entire blame for the Emergency is placed on Mrs Gandhi's shoulders, nothing, it appears, remains to be explained. This perhaps eases our conscience for our own acquiescence in it. It also frees us from self-searching to find whether at some level we too were accomplices in that dastardly development.

But Mrs Gandhi does not explain everything. If it was the sinister ambition of just one person then how was it that few if any in the administration or in her own party and cabinet opposed the move? How was it that the entire business class, intelligentsia and the Press (with rare exceptions) not only dumbly accepted the new order but soon set about discovering non-existent virtues in it? Unlike other dictators, Mrs Gandhi did not have an organised band of fanatics and a vast number among the masses mad after a vision of a future, or economic well-being, or national glory. Her entire strength was derived from the administrative system and an organisation whose only stock in trade had been the promotion in India of a democratic system, whose superiority it paraded over other governments of the third world. How could it be that these instruments fell in line with a dictatorship without demur? It is clear that Mrs Gandhi could not be a convenient peg to hang everything on. One would have to go a little beneath the surface to find the root of the malady.

Much is being said about dismantling the apparatus of dictatorship. But we hardly had an apparatus created. It was the same apparatus, forged over the quarter century of independence with a legacy of the imperial rule, which served Mrs Gandhi in the new role. How can we neglect to examine that apparatus and think of this grand dismantling effort?

The basic aim of the present study is to analyse the developments since independence to discover the sources of the weaknesses of our democratic framework. As much of the country's administration has evolved gradually from the British days, certain salient features of that development too have been touched upon. The main task of the study has been to delineate certain trends. But this task could not be divorced from the denouement of actual events culminating in the Emergency and what followed. So certain developments have been described. However, the study only seeks to sketch an outline of a process.

There is no attempt to go into the details of the excesses of the Emergency or into the resistance that developed against it. No attempt has also been made to go into the details of the underground movement. The author was too close to the underground to find anything heroic about it though certainly there were individuals who showed exceptional courage and dedication. The study of all that, though in great demand, lies beyond the scope of this book.

We have had enough of euphoria. The subject of this study is the thankless job of bringing our people back from that euphoric height to sober reflection on all that has happened. The picture that emerges may be irksome to some important people. But in their own interest and in the interest of us all someone has to hold the mirror. That is one way to prevent a backlash.

It is not just accidental that most of the countries of the third world have slipped into authoritarianism. We are perhaps the longest-surviving democracy in this group. But we too have been treading along the edge of the abyss, and had almost slipped into it. The difficulty in all these countries was that they got a formal structure of democracy without the popular base which alone could sustain it. So one after another they all went down. The fact that our democracy has survived so long, and has even revived from almost a fatal fall, shows that there is some fight left in it. But its survival could not be taken for granted. The popular base has to be built with a certain amount of dedication and willingness to make some sacrifices. The main purpose of the study is to point out the weaknesses of our democratic system so that remedial measures may be devised and enforced.

New Delhi   Sachchidanand Sinha
September 1977

Chapter One

End of an Illusion

.... We have time
To misrepresent, excuse, deny,
Mythify, use this event

W.H. Auden

To a people given over to easy life, interminable talks, imaginative and even fanciful thinking, the Emergency imposed on 26 June 1975, came as a thunder clap. The nation became aware of this unexpected blow through the conspicuous absence of newspapers, most of which failed to appear that morning. Then from foreign radio broadcasts and a few news-sheets hastily rolled off the press which sold within minutes of their publication, people learnt of the imposition of the internal Emergency, the arrest of Mr Jayaprakash Narayan and almost all leaders of the opposition parties, and the imposition of one of the world's most rigorous censorship.

At first people were bewildered. Then bewilderment gave place to panic as people began to be dragged out of bed, from places of their work and from streets to be hauled into prisons. News spread of beatings and tortures and worse: sometimes based on facts, often a pure figment of the mind. Policemen could be found at most street corners in cities, spies were thought to be present everywhere, in fact every stranger next to a person was imagined to be one. Thus a silence descended on a nation of compulsive talkers. Tea houses and coffee houses were still crowded. But people talked in hushed voices when with friends, becoming silent as soon as a stranger approached. And then political talks in cafes stopped altogether as rumour spread that bugging devices had been planted in most of them.

The terror was greater since it imparted an element of surprise to the massive repression. The development of a dictatorship was totally unimaginable to the thinking of most Indians and contrary to the opinions expressed by almost all political leaders since independence. When Mr H.V. Kamath had opposed the inclusion of Emergency clauses in the Indian constitution pointing out that a similar clause in the Weimar constitution of Germany had been used by Hitler to impose his dictatorship through parliamentary means, his fears were lightly brushed aside. The possibility of a parallel situation arising in India was confidently discounted then, and Mr Kamath exclaimed: "God help the people of India!"

Often the prevailing temper of a time is generalised into eternal verities. Most of the men who occupied the august body which framed the constitution trailed behind them the experiences of the freedom struggle, which had at every turning point centred round the question of citizens' rights and liberties. They could not conceive that men following them in government of this country could have less respect for those rights and liberties. It was the nation's opposition to the Rowlatt Act, with its provision of preventive detention and other arbitrary powers, which had led to a massive agitation in the entire country and the massacre of Jalianwalah Bagh in Punjab. No one believed that a national government would contemplate or impose such undemocratic measures in free India. But such hopes were to be belied. In fact, right at the time of the framing of the constitution under pressure of administrative expediency certain freedoms were getting diluted. As it turned out, the tradition of freedom derived from the freedom movement proved a wasting asset.

However, while the character and motivation of men in politics went on changing imperceptibly the values enshrined in the constitution continued to appear inviolate. The people had been so inured to this thought that the myth continued even while facts of life had undergone a sea change. This was the state of mind of the most respectable leaders of the political parties. They were also the ones who were completely stunned when the axe fell. And it is they too who became victims of the greatest fear and despondency. They thought, if what had happened was possible, there could be little hope for the future. They feared the worst without necessarily steeling themselves for the expected disaster.

As the first wave of terror passed, people began to realise what they had lost. Indians had often boasted of their political system, of the superiority of India's democratic institutions over those of the other countries of the third world, most of which had one or other form of authoritarian rule, or even over the institutions of some affluent countries which had given democracy a go-by. Now many foreigners began to taunt Indians for so easily slipping under an authoritarian rule. Even sympathetic Westerners indulged in a bit of self-righteousness pointing to the collapse of the democratic set-up in India. Thus Jack Anderson and Les Whitten in an article published on 4 July 1975 in *Oklahoma Journal* wrote:

> The grasping of dictatorial power by Indira Gandhi, and the acquiescence in this travesty by the Indian establishment, threatening the extinction of democracy in its largest and most challenging setting, will strike thoughtful Americans as a catastrophe of the most mournful kind. Yet it touches a chord of pride in us too. Under similar circumstances Richard Nixon, whatever the sins on his head, never attempted what the sanctimonious Indira has stooped to. Had he done so, no one of significance would have obeyed his orders.

India, which has been among the poorest of the third world countries, lost the one mark of superiority. Freedom appeared to the Indians somehow to make up for lack of prosperity. The sentiment perhaps was in accord with the traditional Indian ethos which alway extolled the value of the spirit over that of material comforts. But the Emergency changed all this. A poor nation was deprived of its pride in freedom—its only ground of self-esteem.

The nineteen nightmarish months since the imposition of the Emergency, during which the citizens were left to the tender mercy of every petty official and policeman, are bound to leave an indelible mark on the psyche of the nation. One good point has been that people have through direct experience learnt the difference between democracy and dictatorship. It certainly should act as an inoculation against growth of dictatorship in the future.

But proverbially public memory is short. As time passes the emotional impact of these dark days will fade away. So will pass away the generation which has seen the happenings of these months. But the underlying forces which brought the dictatorship may remain and be long-lasting, unless consciously eradicated. So it may be dangerous to sit on our laurels. To build a permanent bulwark against a recurrence of dictatorship it is necessary to analyse the situation to discover those elements in our social and political life and tradition which led up to the June events. We must also endeavour to find why our democratic system collapsed so suddenly without a fight. We must look at the events following the Emergency to find out the factors which helped the forces of authoritarianism and those that went against it. They must provide us with lessons for the future.

One illusion is over. But new ones may arise and lead us up to the garden path. What is needed is a hard-headed appraisal of our situation to be able to face it realistically.

Chapter Two

Mixed Bag of Imperial Legacy

Our political system has grown out of an alien graft by the British on our own tradition. The system naturally is heir to all the benefits and the handicaps that have arisen out of this circumstance. Thomas Babington Macaulay, whose ideas shaped a good deal of the imperial educational policy, had proposed to create a class of Indians who in body and blood were Indians, but in taste and temperament English. From 1835 under William Bentinck English education with this motto was launched in India. Finding support from the ideas of Indian reformers like Raja Rammohan Roy, who had set up a syncretic Hindu-European creed in Brahmo Samaj, this policy flourished very well, first in Bengal and then in other parts of British India.

In course of time India developed a colonial elite which had precisely the quality of character outlined by Macaulay. Though numerically small, this elite manned most of the administrative and educational institutions of the British. This also set the ideals and mode of life for the ambitious and aspiring. Subsequently, it was from this elite that the leadership of the nationalist movement was recruited. The character of this elite left a lasting stamp on the politics that evolved in India.

Apart from what the British education imparted to it, certain native factors too went into forming its character. This arose from the fact that this elite was by and large derived from the

upper layers of Indian society both economically and socially—
that is, those recruited to this elite were men who came from
well-to-do families and from the upper castes. Originally they
came mainly from the Brahmins and the Kayasthas who had
formed the class of intellectuals and scribes since very early
periods. This left its own peculiar imprint on the character of
the elite.

Since the British were alien rulers, a handful of men ruling
over a subcontinent, their continued rule depended on impart-
ing to this elite the sense of an inherent superiority of the
former not only of intellect and organisation but also of their
mode of life. As this idea got implanted in the elite it tried to
identify itself more and more with the British rulers and began
also to feel that owing to its British education and association
it was superior to the average Indian. It took meticulous care
to cultivate the manners of the British masters. Incidentally,
this period also coincided with a period of exceptional material
prosperity of the British. Naturally, the style that flourished
reflected the affluence of the British. Since the officials occupy-
ing upper reaches of the administration were paid high salaries,
considering the general poverty of the Indian people, they were
able in some measure to emulate the costly life-style of the
British officers. This created a material gulf between the Indian
people and this elite in addition to the sense of exclusiveness
arising from the new values imparted by the British education.

To this difference was added, as we have noted, the
difference arising from the different economic and social background of the elite and the masses. The rich everywhere suffer
from a sense of inherent superiority. When to their superior
economic background was added superiority of caste and that
arising from English education the chasm became almost un-
bridgeable. Thus the new elitism based on this triple distinction
was to prove a great barrier to the development of the egalitarian ideals of democracy.

Yet there was another factor which led to the separation of
this colonial elite from the people. The British were foreign
rulers and the rhetorics of the 'white man's burden' notwithstanding the empire above everything else had the rather
mundane goal of siphoning off the wealth of the subject peoples

for the benefit of the mother country. Often this process of draining was only thinly disguised as business transaction. Occasionally it took an overtly brutal form giving rise to resentment and resistance. The burden of 'pacifying' the people generally fell on this native elite which formed the bulk of the officialdom and represented, almost in its entirety, that part of it which had to deal directly with the people. Even persons with a deep sense of democratic values would be coarsened towards men if they were frequently to put down people clamouring for justice. But the colonial elite both by training and background even normally could have little sympathy for the common men. The task of maintaining order for the British, often with the help of force, cut whatever bond of sympathy might have remained between them.

This was however true only of those members of the elite who had to perform magisterial or police duties. But a section of the elite also comprised business men, teachers, engineers, lawyers, doctors, and other professional groups. Though sharing in the same value system they were not brutalised to the same extent as the former group. Having to serve the people they could often develop sympathy for them. Thus in spite of its anti-democratic bias there could be isolated men, especially among the professional and teaching groups, who could be sympathetic towards the problems of the people.

This contradiction in the attitude of the elite was heightened by their association with the colonial masters themselves. Closer contacts with the British, preferably through pilgrimage to one of the British universities or to the Inner Temple bar, was an essential pre-requisite for elevation to the status of a *Pucca Sahib*, the highest mark of status in the colonial world. But in this also lay the seeds of fatality for the empire. The latter part of the nineteenth and early part of the twentieth century found the political atmosphere in England permeated by democratic ideals. It was a period when workers and even women were agitating for equal rights and through agitations of various kinds eventually acquired the franchise and many other rights. People talked of economic equality and socialism of a milder kind in England itself and of a more revolutionary kind on the continent, whose echoes often came across the British Channel.

The empire wanted to catch the Indian mind young. But young men who went to qualify in *Sahibdom*, once on the British soil, were caught by new ideals of democracy and equality which were fermenting all round. Besides, the British way of life was marked by a profound sense of liberty and tolerance. It was characterised by a respect for law and severe limitations on the use of arbitrary power of the state against even the meanest individual.

All this was entirely contradictory to the strong-arm policy of the British in India. As a result, as time passed, British ideals led to bitter resentment against British rule or rather the mode of British rule in India in a section of this elite.

However, the prospective bureaucrat-turned-democrat did not have his heart all overflowing with concern for the common man in India. His background and education often fenced him off against all contact with the numerous class of the underdog. What galled him was his own inferior status in comparison with the British citizens whose equal he found himself in every respect. So the fight for freedom, to him, meant above all a fight to regain his self-esteem which had been lost through the subjection of the motherland. When he thought of the people, it was a thought based on some vague sentimental notion. The only people he knew directly were his servants, the sweepers who cleaned his toilet, the *mali* who looked after his garden, or if he was a landlord, his tenants who showed habitual genuflection when he chanced upon them. It was difficult for him to conceive that they were the real people who could ask for equal status and mode of life similar to his own. So the elite's ideals of democracy stood on stilts far above any contact with the dirt and soil of common life.

It was thus that the attempts in the latter part of the nineteenth century to ameliorate the condition of the mill-hands and miners in India attracted unfavourable attention of the nationalist leaders to whom the drain of the resources of an idolised motherland mattered much more than the sufferings of the workers who wasted away in the inhuman conditions of their work. Often the legislations regulating the conditions of work in Indian factories were viewed as a conspiracy to destroy the competitiveness of the Indian industry. This attitude arose not from any malevolence of character but from blindness and incomprehension resulting from the social situation of these leaders.

The privileged were not confined to this English-educated elite, though it occupied the leadership role and set the tone of social life. Among the privileged were also other people such as the traditional rich, the princelings, the new class of landlords created by the British through the permanent settlement and business men who had begun to grow under the new industrial and commercial system, often playing a subsidiary role to British commercial and industrial interests. All these people gradually developed some kind of political and social relationship among themselves. However, inner rivalry and antagonism among them was not absent. But in their social outlook and goal they had a great deal of identity. The under-class of the people comprising the peasants, the industrial workers and the artisans, who were being pauperised progressively, were excluded from the felicities of this holy family of the privileged.

Apart from this division, there was also the division of the castes which in spite of the efforts of several reform movements would not disappear. A large part of the lower castes or *Sudras* were untouchables, any contact with whom was considered polluting by the upper-caste Hindus. They were also the poorest, constituting the bottom layers of society. From generation to generation they toiled in abjectness, leading a precarious existence in normal times, and dying in hordes in times of distress from famine and epidemics. They were practically untouched by what went on in the world of the upper classes. The situation had not much altered when democracy was formally inaugurated in independent India.

Democracy essentially is a system of persuasion, where shift of public opinion or state policy is ensured peacefully. Rule of the majority is only the end-product of this process when periodically people are asked to register their choice. Persuasion requires a free flow of communication among people. And communication in turn is possible only where there is a common language and culture—that is, communication presupposes a modicum of homogeneity in the community.

The elite, with its different tastes, interests, and even language (English had not only become the official language but also the language of refined communication among the elite), superimposed on the traditional social barrier a barrier of its own. However, a democratic system denies any inherent superiority of class or caste. The idea of the equality of man lies at the back of the idea of the equality of the vote. But the elite could not easily unload the burden of its superiority and exclusiveness which also engendered its isolation owing to its past history. Thus while it was inspired by democratic ideals derived from its association with the British political system, its mode of life, again partially derived from the British, militated against those very ideals. This contradiction persists down to this day when India has lived for over a quarter century formally under a democratic system with all the trappings of parties, elections, meetings, and campaigns.

There was also inherent in the mode of life of the elite the tendency to keep it alien to the native people. His style of life was based on the emulation of the style of the West. With independence the craze for the latest Western fashion did not die away. On the contrary, its pace quickened as fashion grew from a water and earth borne to an air-borne disease.

The Western life-style is characterised by newer and newer gadgets as science and technology grows fast and is placed at the disposal of luxury-producing industries. Its economic base, however, is strong enough to sustain the burden of all this conspicuous waste, (though lately environmentalists have begun to cast some doubt on the viability of the system even there). A backward country trying to adopt these gadgets must make itself dependent on the developed economies and transfer a considerable part of its resources to them. Besides, the limited resources of an underdeveloped country would be diverted to acquire those facilities which are needed for the new gadgets rather than to provide for the basic needs of the common people. Thus for example TV transmission stations or motorable roads, or motels would be considered more important than expansion of irrigation facilities or roofs over village schools or even clean drinking water. This creates a basic rift between the priorities of the elite and the priorities of the people.

Elitism is not peculiar to India. But in those countries where the economic base is strong it is possible for the elite to accommodate needs and aspirations of the people also to some extent, as there is a reasonable chance that in time the privileges of the elite would become the common possession of the people in general. Of course, the elite by that time will have acquired other facilities. But the process appears to be on-going and so the system is not threatened. In India where resources were meagre such possibility hardly existed.

As it happened, under the British and long afterwards (in fact right up to this day) administrative services constituted the single largest enterprise where people could get the most lucrative employment. The caste system together with the sense of strong family loyalties operated to proliferate the number of jobs in the administrative service as those already employed sought accommodation for their relations. This created strong vested interests in these jobs.

More and more funds were appropriated through taxation and other means to keep these services in fine fettle. But these services were unproductive and added little to the wealth of the nation. On the other hand, as the repository of the dignity of the state, the departments of the administration vied with each other to acquire more and more pomp and paraphernalia. This further generated an artificial demand in the luxury sector entirely unrelated to the needs of the people. At the same time they pre-empted the resources which could be used to develop the industries catering to the basic needs of the people. Professional and educational services were collateral development of the administrative service and their personnel were inspired by similar ambitions. Thus the immediate needs of the elite militated against the creation of a sound economic base on which alone even a luxury sector could be built in the future.

There was implicit in elitism another dangerous potentiality for the future. With the expansion of families the number of those belonging to the elite grew. This led to the peculiar phenomenon that a person even when lacking the necessary economic or official position could consider himself a member of the elite simply by virtue of his family connection. That would impel him to acquire by fair means or foul the where-withal to maintain an elitist status. Thus the elitist ethos turned out to be the out-branching trunk of nepotism and corruption as the native elite became the rulers of the country. This again eroded the nation's potentiality of growth.

There was also an interesting side-development which we may note in passing. The numerical growth also led many members of the elite to join radical movements. The opportunity to enter the places of profit or power was limited. So many, owing either to lack of inclination or ability of the desired kind, could not join the rat race for offices. In their disillusionment or frustra-tion they sought to undermine the position of their own class or those standing above them by taking up the cause of the masses. This way again they could satisfy their own elitist ego. Extremist politics was more likely to earn instant publicity. At certain stage it also became part of the avant-garde fashion. They could feel their ego amply satisfied when they hit the head-lines. If it brought them nearer to power then it opened up before them a new path leading to the galaxy of the great, which is always the acme of elitist aspirations. In any case, this did not fall in the general line of the elitist development and was a countervailing influence on the parasitic role of the elite.

However inimical to the public interest, the elite always had the controlling hand in the management of the economy. This would gradually create disillusionment among the people about the democratic process through which the whole opera-tion was conducted. They consequently tended to look with suspicion on all political professions. They alternated between long spells of apathy and sudden spurt of fury sometimes leading to violent actions. The general anaemia that we wit-nessed in our political life was thus made inevitable.

But the kind of contradiction to which we have drawn at-tention lay dormant so long, as the chief pre-occupation was freedom from the foreign yoke. It always happens that the dominant classes beguile themselves into the belief that their own interest is the interest of the entire people. The leaders of the nationalist movement in India too quite innocently thought that what appeared most desirable to them must also appear desirable to the whole nation. Since they were the opinion leaders of society, for a while they would make people look at the world though their glasses. In any case the contradiction could hardly surface unless these leaders were called upon to deal with concrete socio-economic problems with the winning of independence and democratic rights.

So, in spite of the seeds of contradiction the nationalist movement was able to mobilise a sizeable part of the population in its struggle to wrest freedom from the British government. This process certainly was helped by the nature of the government in Great Britain itself. Since the British had a liberal and democratic order in their own country, in response to the agitation in India, in the British Parliament itself there was pressure to grant some of those freedoms to the Indian subjects that the British enjoyed at home. The Government of India Acts of 1919 and 1935 were the results of this kind of pressure.

The British economic and global political interests in India were very vital and so, barring a handful of idealists, Labour leaders and the Conservatives were equally united in their denial of full independence to India. But through the interaction of the above kind a structure of popular participation at lower levels of administration was built and the concept of the rule of law, and within limits freedom of expresson, freedom of the Press and the right to organise trade unions and political parties were established. The federal nature of the Indian state too in its rudiments evolved under British rule itself. However, the principle of adult suffrage had never been accepted not even under the Government of India Act of 1935. The franchise was limited by property and educational qualifications.

But whatever the merit of these schemes of popular participation, it was appended to the hierarchic rule of the officialdom that obtained at the time of their introduction. There were local self-governments which managed some public services. But the pivotal role in the administration was played by the district collector. He was responsible for nearly every kind of administrative development, revenue and relief work in the

district. He had a hierarchy of officials under him down to
the village level. He had also the police force of the district
under his control. The elected representatives who manned
the municipalities or the district boards could not interfere
with his overall administrative control and had to operate within
restricted fields.

This feature of the Indian political system persisted even
after independence when a democratic constitution was brought
into operation. This has left an in-built anti-democratic bias in
the Indian administrative system. The district collector is beyond the control of any local authority and representative.
He is directly under the State ministry and in fact under certain circumstances can at the bidding of the authorities in New
Delhi through the Governor act even against the State ministers or be beyond their control. Grudgingly, in normal times
he submits to the authority of the elected government of the
State. But he is often ready to humiliate the elected representatives should an opportunity arise. The democratic system has
failed so far to tame the elitist temper in the civil servants.

Even though the rights of the people were thus hemmed in
by several qualifications and stratagem, the principle at least
had been accepted that the Indians should in fullness of time
enjoy all those rights which are due under a fully democratic
order.

The above factors were the positive side of the British legacy.
On the negative side were those factors which were inseparable
from an alien rule, which must in the last analysis rest on
naked force. The most durable result of this aspect of the
foreign rule was that the bureauracy and the police force were
kept wholly estranged from the people. A policeman's ideal
under the system was to create and sustain a condition where
people feared him. It was generally believed that the capacity
of the police force to keep the people in awe of its authority
was the best guarantee against any crime and in particular
against the worst crime of all—sedition against the imperial
rule. To achieve this end the police were given almost a free
hand to bludgeon a person or to bundle him into prison on the
slightest provocation or often without any provocation at all.
Breaking the bones of an alleged criminal or even branding

him to extract a confession or a clue to crime was not frowned upon. In fact, such excesses had become an indispensable ingredient of criminal investigation.

The deep division of society added its own nuance to this barbaric order. The influential and the rich people could often appeal against such treatment, taking resort to the written laws. To the poor the word of the local police official became the final command of law. They could be mutilated or even murdered in police custody with little chance of intercession or even investigation on their behalf. The ostracism of those belonging to the lowest and the poorest castes was also reflected in the criminal code. In it entire tribes or castes of people were declared as criminal and their members were duty-bound to keep the police officials informed of their whereabouts with liability of punishment in case of failure. There was provision also to haul up a poor person and to put him in jail merely for surviving without any ostensible means of livelihood. A landless agricultural worker who had no permanent employment could be made a victim of this law any time he displeased a police officer.

But apart from these institutions, the British system also left the legacy of an excessive concern for the stability and order in the political system. In the present Indian context this concern often appears irrational. In a society, which has a reasonable rate of growth, assuring even to the poorest continuous improvement in the standard of living, a disruption in the political and economic system may mean substantial material loss. But in a society marked by stagnation or impoverishment of a sizeable segment of the population, which is chronically undernourished or starved owing to great inequalities, stability could be beneficial only to the few who have a vested interest in such a system. But in India this concern for stability persisted and all responsible leaders have accepted this faith in stability above everything else. Perhaps it again reflects the attitude of a privileged minority.

This attitude influenced not only the framing of the constitution, which had riders to every right accorded to the people, but also in the development of the party system and government in the country. Even radical leaders would quail at the insinuation that their action was likely to cause instability. And however misconceived, to many people stability has been synonymous with a system where the command from the top is obeyed without demur by all lower down.

Chapter Three

The Drift

I

While the constitutional development since the latter part of British rule was moving in the direction of democratisation, the socio-economic conditions and the administrative system worked as halters on this development. However, the severest strain on the democratic system arose from the climate of insecurity and fanaticism resulting from the partition of the country and the communal holocaust that engulfed a large part of the country. This brought to the fore all forces of authoritarianism latent in the system.

Even in normal times democracy is a difficult and, for the rulers, the most inconvenient system to work. Its survival depends on the willingness of those running the system to endure a great deal of what is irritating and obnoxious in their opponents. Often its values have to be defended at great personal risk or even risk to the system itself. From the moment the rulers' judgment is dictated by their personal likes and dislikes or convenience, they move down an inclined plane. Soon fancies would appear as facts and criticism as subversion. When the rulers appear in their own eyes in the role of saviours of the integrity of the nation, preservation of their own rule tends to be identified with the preservation of the nation itself. Intolerance towards opponents may then begin to assume the aura of unflinching determination to defend the nation.

Defending the nation against communal riots and possible
disintegration resulting therefrom created some such self-
appraisal in the nationalist leaders.

The communal riots and partition threatened the newly-
created democratic order from two sides. On the one hand it
instilled communal exclusiveness among the two major communities of the country. The Hindus considered the Muslims
the chief instrument of the nation's partition and as such
became suspicious of their loyalty to the nation. The Muslims
laboured under a different kind of suspicion which arose from
a sense of helplessness, guilt and fear. They had by and large
voted for the partition of the country. But the division of the
country left them more isolated and vulnerable than before.
Besides, at the back of their mind they had the feeling that
since they had worked for the partition there was bound to be
retaliation from the dominant community. This psychological
situation gave great sustenance to communal groups and parties which by creating communal exclusiveness in the population weakened the process of polarisation on a rational basis.
The Hindus turned in large numbers towards the militant
chauvinism of the RSS. The Muslims in panic rallied round
the Muslim League which had outlived its political usefulness
but still appeared to offer a protective umbrella.

As a counterpart of this alienation of large sections of
political opinion from the main stream of the national movement was the belief among the Congress leaders that they were
the sole custodians of India's nationhood and sovereignty.
The Congress and the groups allied to it had a genuine fear
that the nation was threatened with disintegration. The nation
had been divided, the entire northern India was ablaze with
communal passion, the future of the princely states remained
uncertain and to cap it all Gandhi, whose one-man mission
appeared the only hope to balm the nation's distemper, was
murdered in early 1948. There was plenty of excuse, if the
leaders of newly-formed Congress government needed any, to
be ruthless in dealing with the problems they faced.

It was at this time that RSS workers were arrested in large
numbers and their overt activities stopped. There is little doubt
that the RSS had a hand in fanning the flames of communalism

during the early days of independence. It openly challenged the secular foundation of the nation. For all this it deserved condemnation by everyone who held the welfare of people at heart. However, to fight their poisonous influence the battle had to be joined for the minds and hearts of the people. But it was characteristic of the new rulers that they chose the path of arrest and repression of a movement whose appeal was deeply emotional. As subsequent events were to show the police measures succeeded merely in driving the movement underground. It hibernated for a few months only to emerge with new vigour. In fact, it had strong sympathisers in the administration who lent it all kinds of support.

But the rulers' handling of the RSS was kid-gloved compared to their handling of the communists and especially of the Telengana peasant movement, which erupted almost on the heels of the transfer of power. It was the period when the Indian constitution was being framed. Attempts were being made to integrate the princely states of India in the Indian Union. Even though many inducements were provided to the princes, Hyderabad was proving recalcitrant. Encouraged by the Nizam the Razakars, who were a militant armed group, did some muscle-flexing to impress the world with their determination to resist integration with India. However, they disintegrated as soon as the Indian forces swooped on Hyderabad in a 'Police Operation.' But the real brunt of the police operation had to be borne by the peasants of Telengana who had been in ferment for some time and were settling accounts with their landlords and other oppressors. Incidentally, their operation also was then in line with the new strategy of the Communist Party of India to create guerrilla base areas on the pattern of China. To these peasants the taste of the new nationhood was bitter. Soon after the integration of Hyderabad with India the peasant revolt was drowned in blood by the Indian forces. About this operation Durga Das writes:

Patel launched a powerful attack on the disruptionists both of the left and the right. He ruthlessly crushed the communist revolt in Telengana in Hyderabad State with the help of the hand-picked officials. He ordered the police to shoot at sight and kill as many rebels as was necessary to break the back of the uprising. As a result of the directive, over a thousand persons were shot dead and the communist extremists were so demoralised that for the next two decades they eschewed armed action and took to constitutional means.[1]

Over a thousand persons killed in a small region did not seem to cause any concern in the country. Perhaps people did not know much as to what was happening. Maybe the concern for the integrity of the nation-state was so overwhelming that loss of lives of nation's own citizens did not count for much. But more likely because those who were the opinion leaders of society did not bother since those killed were poor peasants and tribals whose citizenship was a mere formality in an elitist world. The nation was getting insensitised for the things to come later. Subsequently, for over the best part of a quarter century the nation's armed forces carried on a relentless war against the tribal peoples of Nagaland and Mizoram. The only fault of these hapless tribals being a determination to maintain their identity which they feared would be lost in a big nation if they surrendered their autonomy. But again much of this action went not only unchallenged but even met with approbation, presumably because the enlightened public opinion seriously felt that the few hundred thousand people living in the isolation of their mountainous abodes posed a serious threat to the security of the nation.

The excessive concern for the integrity of the nation following the events during and after the transfer of power so warped the imagination of even men of vision that they were willing to make such concessions to the central government as were likely to place serious curbs on the freedom of the citizens or on the autonomy of the States in a federal set-up. Mr Jayaprakash Narayan himself among others had made the following suggestion for incorporation in the constitution to the Drafting Committee of the Constituent Assembly in 1948:

[1]Du ga Das : *India from Curzon to Nehru and After*, Collins, London 1969, p. 28.

40860

(c) If public safety and order be seriously disturbed in any part of the Republic and the Government of the State concerned fails to restore public order, the President of the federation may restore public safety and order with the help of armed forces. Under such circumstances all authorities of the State concerned shall assist and obey the instructions of the executive authority of the federation and its duly authorised agents in the restoration of public safety.

(d) If public safety and order be seriously disturbed the executive authority of the federation may also suspend the provisions of the constitution concerning freedom of speech, association and assembly and inviolability of person, home and correspondence in the manner and to the extent determined by the federal law for such occasion.[1]

It is interesting to note that these proposals were not very different from the ones incorporated in the 42nd amendment to the constitution rushed through during the Emergency. The new article 257A inserted in the constitution under the 42nd amendment reads:

(1) The Government of India may deploy any armed force of the Union or any other force subject to the control of the Union for dealing with any grave situation of law and order in any State.

(2) Any armed force or other force or any contingent or unit thereof deployed under clause (1) in any State shall act in accordance with such directions as the Government of India may issue and shall not, save as otherwise provided in such direction, be subject to the superintendence or control of the State Government or any officer or authority subordinate to the State Government.

---

[1]Quoted in the *Framing of India's Constitution*, Vol IV, Edited by B. Shiva Roa, The Indian Institute of Public Administration, New Delhi, p. 364.

069651

Also it would be noted that all the draconian powers taking away the liberties of the citizen which were in operation during the Emergency were recommended in clause (d) of Mr Jayaprakash Narayan's proposals.

But the demand for greater power for the Union and greater punitive power against the citizens was not always based on a selfless concern for the integrity of the national state. Often it reflected the concern to curb radical movements. Especially the vested interests clamoured for strong action against labour movement and particularly the communists who then were taking a radical political line. As early as March 1948 the Communist Party was banned in West Bengal. By August 1949 thousands of communists were arrested all over the country. Following Bengal, the Communist Party was banned in Madras, Mysore, Hyderabad, Travancore, Cochin, Indore, Bhopal and Chandernagar. Its newspapers were banned in several States. Raids on its offices were carried out to seize men and literature, and with the added purpose of creating a sense of terror among its workers.

In a swoop in March 1949 hundreds of Railway workers were arrested all over the country to prevent the Railway strike in response to a breakaway section of the Railwaymen's Federation under the leadership of the Communist Party. All this happened but no voice of protest was raised except by victims of the measures.

Trade union movement as a whole was later to receive a raw deal. Introduction of machinery for compulsory arbitration, declaration of certain industries as essential services and illegalising strikes in them, and through other punitive measures strikes in any major industry were made virtually impossible. This led to the attenuation of the capacity of the workers to defend their rights through the use of their own organised strength.

The move against the communists was only the thin end of the wedge. Predictably, the extraordinary powers assumed by the executive in the name of dealing with subversion were used against other opponents of the ruling party as occasion arose.

In February 1950 Preventive Detention Act was passed,

which empowered the government to arrest a person on suspicion and to detain him without trial. We have already seen
how the Rowlatt Act, which gave similar powers to government
when introduced in 1919 by the British government, was met
with stiff resistance by the entire nationalist movement. But
now a similar black Act was introduced by the same nationalist leaders in the name of the integrity of the nation. Soon
trade unionists, socialists and people of other radical persua-
sions were arrested under it.

Similarly police firings against demonstrations of the workers and peasants became a common feature of Indian political
life. In the beginning the shooting down of the people was
defended in the name of the integrity of the national state. In
the fifties when Mr Morarji Desai was the Chief Minister of
composite Bombay State hundreds of men were shot down under
his orders to defend the integrity of the multi-lingual State
against the agitation for linguistic States. Now men began to
be shot to defend anything—even an electric pole or a garbage
can. The only defenceless entity was the citizen, the sovereign
of the nation, especially so if he happened to be poor.

Acts of unrestrained power are often initiated to defend
some high principle. But such acts rarely remain a one-time
exception. So the unrestrained and irresponsible use of police
power gathered momentum with time.

Things appeared to be getting too far when Dr R.M.
Lohia tried to cry a halt in mid-fifties. He wanted his own
party to set an example so as to arrest this devaluation of
human life in free India. He was the General Secretary of the
Praja Socialist Party whose member headed the ministry in
Kerala. There was a police firing in Kerala resulting in loss
of a few lives. He directed the Praja Socialist ministry to
institute a judicial enquiry into the firing and to resign. He
held that human life is too precious a thing to be left to the
whims of officialdom, and the steps he had suggested he
thought would lead to greater circumspection in future while
using force against the people. He also wanted to lay down
certain principles clearly setting down the conditions under
which alone police should be allowed to resort to firing. He
did not think that destruction of property constituted sufficient

provocation for firing. He on the other hand felt that firing could be justified only when a mob had already killed some one and was likely to cause more deaths. Unless this was done much police firing tended to be preventive killing; something worse than preventive detention.

The reaction of his party colleagues was revealing of the attitude of the political elite in this country. Most of his party colleagues, including the Chairman of the Praja Socialist Party Acharya Kripalani and a lifelong associate Mr Jayaprakash Narayan, turned against him in the controversy that followed his suggestions. Of course, the ministry did not resign and at the party convention held to decide the issue Lohia lost, though with his incisive argument he rendered most of his opponents speechless. It was becoming evident that the politicians in India did not care much for principles so long as they had a finger in the till.

This insensitivity to human life again emanated from our peculiar social situation. In a country where poor men form the overwhelming majority the value of property or the things that constitute property must be held higher than the value of human life if the institution of private property and privileges were to survive. A political leadership either committed to safeguarding property or having roots in the privileged strata of the population could not be expected to show excessive regard for the lives of the poor. But shooting was not the only weapon in the service of repression. Large-scale arrests, detention without trial, beatings and torture of political prisoners were some other methods employed to serve the same aim.

This aplomb of the leaders of the political parties towards police excesses and their refusal to restructure the whole machinery of law and order may be contrasted with the following observations of a former Inspector General of Police and Secretary of the first Police Commission appointed in independent India by the Government of Bihar:

After the Quit India movement, the British Government favoured greater militarisation of the police force, a process which has found particular favour since 1950. When I was attached to Scotland Yard, I was pleasantly surprised to see that British Police did not carry any firearms. Even when some of them were shot dead on duty, they refused to arm themselves. The opposite is the case in this land of Buddha and Gandhi. The police continue to use the third degree as a short-cut to successful investigation. There is no reason why barbarous methods should be used, especially when there has been remarkable progress in forensic science. It is only when they do not use their intelligence that they have to use dubious methods, and in some cases this may even result in murder.[1]

But a political leadership intrinsically suspicious of the people could not easily discard its coat of mail bequeathed by an imperial predecessor.

After the Sino-Indian war the left communists (later CPM) became a special object of attention for the guardians of public order. A large number of their workers and supporters were rounded up and detained under the Defence of India Rules. It is to be recalled that the Defence of India Rules is part of our British heritage. However, there is a difference. The British invoked the DIR only in times of war. But in independent India it is tending to become a permanent feature of our administrative system.

In 1965 the nation was in ferment and students, workers, peasants and many other sections of the population were agitating for different demands. Once again the DIR was used in a big way to arrest most of the active or inactive workers of the left parties. The largest number of workers arrested this time perhaps belonged to the SSP. Now the socialists and communists were sailing in the same boat. The irony of the situation was that many socialists previously had supported the arrest of the communists. Even as late as 1965 Mr N.G. Goray, the then Chairman of the Praja Socialist Party, came up with the demand to ban the left Communist Party. The SSP, of course, had changed its policy on this issue by now. The Swatantra and the Jana Sangh had always pleaded for

---

[1]M.K. Sinha, "Palice Problems," published in *Statesman*, 2 July 1977.

the banning of the Communist Parties. The communists paid in kind and demanded the banning of the Jana Sangh when they found themselves on the right side of the ruling party.

When in 1959 the Congress government at the Centre took the extraordinary step of dismissing the communist ministry in Kerala even though the latter enjoyed a clear majority in the legislature the step was applauded by almost the entire non-communist opposition. Predictably the general people showed little concern when the Centre moved in the same manner to dismiss other State ministries formed by non-Congress parties.

It has been a curious feature of India's political life in the post-independence era that parties accused each other of authoritarian intent, and in their concern to save democracy demanded just those remedies which were likely to promote authoritarianism. While the accusations were often far-fetched, originating either in rhetorical flourish or polemic, the remedies suggested were real and instilled among the general public a sense of apathy towards anti-democratic actions of the state.

The confusion of ideas as to the mode of of operation in a democratic polity and had made its most tragic manifestation in West Bengal since 1967. A ministry led by the CPM began by making short work of tolerance among political workers. Even the coalition partners were not spared. Of course the plea was that when class war was on class enemies could not for long remain political allies. The situation sometimes was embarrassing to the leaders, but the rank and file who were indoctrinated in certain extremist ideology could not easily be held back. But parliamentary politics has its limitations. As long as there were constitutional and legal restrains it could not be a free for all. Besides, the CPM only headed a coalition so it had to operate within certain restraints. The CPM split up and a new phenomenon, Naxalism, erupted on India's political horizon. Now annihilation of all and sundry as class enemy became the order of the day. Often the poorest and the most backward strata of the population, which through default or deliberation had been kept out of the political process, found expression in the kind of elemental violence this movement encouraged. The violence escalated. This was countered by the terror campaign of the police. They arrested, tortured and

killed any one on the slightest suspicion of Naxalite association. The regular toughs took a hand too. They joined the
youth wing of the Congress or any other political group according to their convenience and wreaked their own kind of venge-
ance. Violence had taken command of every aspect of political
life so completely that the CPM was forced in the Assembly
election of 1972 to abandon many of its constituencies and as a
protest against what it called unfair elections, it staged a boycott of the Assembly. Bengal was already far on the road to
authoritarian rule and this system was only waiting for the
imprimatur of the legal authority in New Delhi to envelop
the whole country.

But the use of physical violence and constraints was not the
only means at the disposal of the government and the ruling
classes to keep the people in their places. A more important
influence was exercised through misinformation and blackout
of such news as would expose the injustice of the system. In
theory and as far as formalities go the Press in India was free.
One could write and publish anything except that which attracted the law of libel. But it was only a theoretical possibility.
In actual fact one's writing was limited by what the editors
were willing to publish. It was a major qualification. Most of
the large and influential newspapers were owned and controlled
by business houses. And the editors had often to express the
views of the proprietors. Even nationally known editors could
be sacked by the owners without much ceremony.

Since in India business interests depended to a great extent
on the favour of the government, the newspapers had a tilt in
favour of the ruling party too. However, it must be conceded
that it was merely a tilt, not total subservience. Whenever a
pronounced favour was shown, it was to the interest of the
owners rather than to that of the government.

Another factor which influenced the policy of the Press was
advertisement. No major newspaper can run without advertisements. But the substantial advertisers were either the large
business houses or the government departments. The two
together worked to the detriment of the opposition parties
professing radical policies. Experience also shows that neither
the government (in the States or at the Centre) nor the business

men showed any respect for the freedom of the Press. Whenever the newspapers earned their displeasure, advertisements
would be affected. *The Times of India* had to experience such
pressure quite early when Mr Morarji Desai was the Chief
Minister of Bombay. Owing to some displeasure with its policies the Bombay Government stopped its advertisements to it.
This was probably among the earliest examples of arm-twisting
of a newspaper by the government. But such occurrences
became numerous as time wore on.

In the name of showing concern for small newspapers the
government later tried openly to buy their favour by offering
them advertisements. Lacking their own resources these newspapers became so totally dependent on the largesse of the
government that they could not but toe the official line in most
matters.

It has to be conceded, however, that in spite of the heavy
odds the Press in India did often give expression to the feelings
of the people. Within limits it had also attained a level of
objective reporting, But in a country with a low percentage of
literacy the newspaper's role in spreading information and
influencing people's views was limited. It is the All India
Radio whose broadcasts in all the national and regional langua-
ges reach the remotest village in the country. It is one
agency which caters for the largest number of people. And
this agency remained completely under the control of the
the central government. In spite of repeated demands to turn
it into an autonomous corporation so as to make the presenta-
tion of news and views more impartial it continued to be the
monopoly of the ruling party. With the passage of time the
All India Radio became more and more an instrument of mass
regimentation in favour of those in power.

Thus in full view of those leaders who professed to stand
for democracy the administrative system was developing the
attitudes and instruments of an authoritarian rule. Owing to
their different compulsions at one stage or another most of the
leaders wittingly or unwittingly lent their hand to this process.

II

Democracy inherently is a great equaliser. Given a free play it would permit no system of privileges or more glaring kind of social or economic disability to survive for long. The reason is simple. As the democratic system evolves, giving rise to serious contention for power, and as the strengths of the main contenders get evenly matched even small groups begin to assume importance in tipping the scale one way or the other. Thus politics gradually shifts to the door-steps of even those who have remained relegated to the backwaters of society. As the contending parties try to woo even the smallest groups whose support tends to be decisive, the latter's demand begins to occupy the main stage of politics. Thus in course of time such groups move from the passive to the active stage of enfranchisement. It is true that this happens only when the group in question has become self-conscious and aware of its problems. But it does not have to wait long for such consciousness to arrive. Since the parties themselves approach the people with all kinds of alluring promises they soon spark hope among them and also make them conscious of their inadequacies.

But this basic trait of democracy may prove destructive to the fragile base of the privileged and the elite which also happens to be the foster-father of the democratic system in the country. This has created an awe of the common mass and its elemental potentiality. To the less sophisticated members of our elite even the extension of the franchise to the illiterate appears a vulgarisation of the democratic process. Even the demand to introduce some educational qualification for the right to vote is aired at times. But to the more sophisticated such remedies are not only too crude but militate against their democratic profession. To contain this subterranean force, to circumscribe it, the political leadership has intuitively sought other more subtle subterfuge. Besides, it has developed fixations about certain formal structure and process of the democratic system.

This attitude has prevented the evolution of a recruitment system for the bureaucracy and the higher echelons of the armed forces and the police in a direction where they could draw closer to the people. It has kept the old administrative system intact which puts the bureaucracy up to the district level (as we have alreary noted) securely in command, with the elected representatives having virtually no say in its affairs. It keeps the educational system on two tiers, one for the elite and the other for the masses with the fewest possibilities of entry from the second to the first. Since entry to the highest ranks of the civil, police and military services depends on a certain kind of educational standard, best developed in the special public and military schools, entry to these services is barred to the lower classes who cannot send their childern to these special schools either owing to financial reasons or the needs of preparatory education beyond their means. In fact, to the poorest even education of an inferior kind is not easily accessible.

In this way the elite secures in its hands those levers of effective control which could be used to counter the 'excesses' of democracy, i.e., when the masses strain to get out of hand.

But with the expanding base of democracy all this could prove but poor security. So the formal aspects of democracy itself had to be so structured as to direct it through safe channels. This required certain conditions to be laid at the outset as axiomatic. One such condition is rooted in the fetish of stability. Stability often means stability of a given system of relationships, which invariably has, in our present world, embedded within it a certain class of privileges. But people who are defending some vested interests of their own would not easily admit even to themselves that they are doing so. Their aims are camouflaged in some such disjunctive affirmation as: freedom yes, instability never. With such false dichotomy one could easily beguile oneself and others about the real issues involved.

A little objective thinking will show, however, that the claims of stability like the claims of integrity are claims affecting the interests of those who hold power and privilege. A dictatorship expanding its area of control or attaining a degree of stability does not benefit the victims of its rule. Nor does a democratic capitalist system expanding its rule over tribal people benefit either its own citizens or the tribals. It is true about any such system based on privileges.

In fact, the stability of a system characterised by large organisations only renders it less responsive to the demands of the ordinary citizens. If we examine the condition of the people or their rights during the past decade, we would find that the government at the Centre became responsive to them precisely in the years when it was least stable. This was for example, the situation in 1969-70 when after the Congress split Mrs Indira Gandhi's government at the Centre had a precarious majority. It was during this period too that for the first time the law for preventive detention was allowed to lapse. Also it was around this time that maximum concessions were made to the demands of the workers and other weaker sections of the population. After 1971 we had a very stable government. But this period also saw the gradual erosion of people's rights culminating finally in the dictatorship of 1975-76.

One way in which stability of the system was sought was to emphasise the need for a two-party system. As its operation has shown in some countries it helps to keep political differences within narrow bounds. As the system gets stabilised entry for new interests seeking radically to alter existing relations becomes somewhat difficult. They have to ally themselves with one or the other of the major parties, which they can do only by accepting the basic framework of their ideology. Though this does not wholly exclude a radical element from the system it includes it after watering down to some extent its revolutionary fervour. This can certainly delay if not prevent the incursion of radical politics. This is very obvious in the United States and Great Britain where two-party system has weathered many stormy periods of history without allowing radicalism to acquire any foothold. Whether it arose in sheer naivety or was a rationalisation of the fear of radicalism, the dogma of the two-party system has been accepted by all the important political parties excepting the communists who in any case dispute the sanctity of the parliamentary system itself.

The stability of the democratic process, however, is not directly related to the two-pary system. In many of the European countries such as Sweden, Switzerland, and Denmark a very stable democratic system has thrived with multiplicity of parties.

But it is true too that in a multiple-party system chances of a new party shooting into prominence from obscurity on the wave of a new mass movemett is much greater. However, in a country where the whole economic structure is very fluid and discontent among the people deep, privileged people like to freeze existing political relations. So to serve this end an unreal argument was built about the merits of the two-party system. The real reason for the stability of the democratic system in some of the Western countries, whether with two or multiparty system was their sound economic base. This could offer reasonable security of livelihood and welfare to most of their citizens. This kept the loyalty of the majority of the citizens unshaken through all the vicissitudes of fortunes of the various parties.

If in India the development of such a stable two-party system has remained a pious wish it is because the discrepancies between the demands of the two major constituents of its polity (the elite and the mass) are too great to be easily accommodated in such a harmonious relation of two parties. The parties of the privileged or the leaders of the various parties which are derived from the privileged strata are too similar to lead to a political polarisation. On the other hand, the poor are so poor and their demands are so incomprehensible to the elite that a party representing mainly their interests would not get the respectability to qualify for the status of a proper democratic party. Possibly such a party would appear subversive to decency, education, intellect and all that goes to make a cultured life. And this would not be surprising because the poor people in this land have been deprived nearly of all this till now.

The leaders of the accredited political parties are monotonously similar. This is reflected in the fluidity of their membership and leadership. They gravitate too easily towards power. This is amply shown by the widespread defection from the parties. This problem has remained at the core of the political life of India and bedevils the evolution of a healthy democratic system.

This contradiction often gives rise to two extreme reactions to the system. On the one hand, irritated by the pressing demands of the poor the vested interests seek to limit or destroy the democratic process by narrowing the area of mass action or participation in it. On the other hand, frustrated by the delays and hurdles in getting even the smallest concession to their demand, some sections of the poorest people try to break loose from the electoral process and seek redressal of their grievances through more direct extra-parliamentary channels. Of course, the first is easier to accomplish as there is inherently an anti-people bias in the system. The vested interests can operate without interfering with the system in any ostensible way. The aspiration of the people is more difficult to realise through an extra-parliamentary process, as the military-bureaucratic control is quite effective and in any revolt the scattered and ill-organised strength of the people is pitched against a highly centralised and effectively organised force of the state. In fact attempts of the latter type give an excuse to the vested interests to secure a stronger foothold in the state apparatus and to push it more in the anti-democratic direction.

Social events are too complex to be explained in terms of a single causal relation. But the two extremes of sporadic eruption of violence among the people on the one hand and extra-legal summary execution of leftist militants by the police on the other, which became a part of Bengal polity as already noted, certainly owe their origin in some measure to this contradiction in our political life. Bengal, which came earliest under the influence of the new system of English education, also displayed in a more acute form this social division. Calcutta, as the seat of imperial power and the new culture implanted along with the new education, had become a strong magnet to all those who aspired to what was then conceived as cultured life. Not only those who had jobs in Calcutta but even those belonging to the landed gentry converged on the city in search of enlightened life. This created a numerous class of absentee landlords living in and around Calcutta whose luxurious culture thrived on the drain of the resources of the village and people actually engaged in agricultural operation. While the new life-style in the city flourished, agriculture stagnated resulting in the great impoverishment of the peasants and the agricultural workers. Democratic political life with its high polish remained a preserve of the city-bred leaders. To the villager the cumbersome, often time-taking and materially sterile politics of elections appeared as empty ritual. When a section of the disillusioned or disgruntled elite appeared with a vision of instant justice to this rural mass it found eager ears. The peasants would be easily persuaded to set right with their own organised strength what the legislatures promised without ever settling down to implement. This was the key factor behind the genesis of the extremist movement whatever the ideological patina its friends or enemies might have put on it.

This was the kind of constraints under which the democratic system had to work in the whole country. It is the compulsion of democratic politics that the appeal be made to the interests of the largest number. But in the very nature of things this appeal was to be hollow. Often the elite, which formed the leadership of all the political parties, found it hard to comprehend the problems that really exercised the mind of the common man. Often when the elite sought solution of these problems he found his position threatened. Elaborate plans would be drawn up with sincerity for social reforms. But such plans met with an invisible resistance when they came up for implementation. At this stage the whole administrative machinery would appear to be working to slow them down or sabotage them. This has been the experience with most land-reform measures, measures to curtail luxuries or tax the rich or measures to expand and bring up the level of education among the weaker sections of the population.

But to get a foothold among the people, even from purely selfish ends, the political parties were required to look to their problems. Attempts were made too to organise the people in villages for some political action. But as the luxuries in the cities grew and a large number of political workers began to share these through a system of patronage, the enthusiasm to go to the rural masses cooled down. The villages were getting impoverished day by day. Their life appeared increasingly insipid compared to what the cities had to offer. But even in the cities the poorest were not looked after too well. The city slums looked even worse in contrast to the affluent parts of the city. To live in them and to work there was plainly degrading.

So the competition grew for the few places which could offer the benefaction of nearness to power. Political workers crowded the cities and towns and a cut-throat competition ensued for the few places of profit which the political apparatus could offer. As this led to greater alienation from the people, the faith in the masses declined.

The new attitude found expression in the philosophy that in India nothing could be accomplished from outside political power. This led to the belief among some that even the hunger for reform among the masses could be roused only by bestowing some benefits on them from the seats of power. The sequel was the search for areas of co-operation with the ruling party. Thus many of the leaders, who originally advocated the building up of a strong opposition to the ruling Congress, were convinced now that any change in this country could be brought about only through the policy-shifts within the ruling party itself. Defection to the ruling party now gained a high polish of principle leading to a mass exodus from the opposition. This further weakened whatever little challenge there had been to the ruling party to look to the problems of the people.

The many attempts to unify the various political parties were only a counterpart of the defection to the ruling party. The rumps of the various political parties, which represented the more deeply committed members or those who could not find comfortable berths in the ruling party, found in unity of the parties the only chance to get anywhere near power. So every electoral reverse or critical change in the political situation set in motion moves for unification of opposition parties. A bid to get into power could take one of two forms: (1) the attempt to go to the people to work among them with greater vigour so as to win their support in an election; or (2) to present a united face which could look formidable and convincing even when it lacked any real strength behind it. The first owing to the reasons already discussed could not be countenanced. So only the second course could find favour.

The pathetic attempt to make up for mass support by patch-up attempts at the top was very conspicuous in the

Socialist Party, the only non-communist party which believed in mass movement and basic social transformation. The socialists, who had worked among the workers and peasants, since the early fifties, began to find that the work was not very rewarding politically. Trade union work was not easily convertible into an electoral dividend. The work among the peasants was too demanding. Besides, after the Zamindari abolition and the few other tenancy reforms the socialist leaders in the villages, who themselves came from relatively better off farming families, lost the appetite for work among the poorest sections of the village population. Many socialists in the beginning had been Marxists and had with great zeal accepted the idea of declassing themselves. But the call of creature comforts, which governmental patronage was bringing to a section of the political activists, began to cast its spell on them.

Now political workers were getting declassed in the reverse order. Even those who came from modest backgrounds learnt to live in comforts copying the life-style of those who had acquired some prosperity. As only a few of the political workers could afford to lead such a life on the basis of their own financial resources, corruption of various kinds began to spread among them. Thus there was a decline in their mass support. Dr Lohia tried to infuse a certain kind of militancy in the ranks of the socialists but it was sporadic and did not lead to any sustained work among the masses. However, he was able to arrest for a while the growing aptitude for luxury among the socialist workers. He was able also to give for the first time a new orientation to socialist policy in the direction of bridging the gulf between the elite and the masses by his emphasis on a uniform system of education and people's language. Though this created a band of dedicated workers, it also isolated him from the dominant current of political opinion. So his following remained small. After his death in 1967 most of his followers also fell in line with the general trend.

Attempts to shore up the sagging strength of the Socialist Party, which wanted to become the alternative to the Congress, resulted in a series of fusions and fissions. In the beginning the PSP was formed with the amalgamation of the Socialist Party

and the Kisan Mazdoor Party which was a breakaway group
of the Congress. Then the party broke up again on the issue
of police firing (to which we have already referred) to give
birth to the PSP and the Socialist Party. Subsequently a merger
of a section of the former with the latter resulted in the formation of the Samyukta Socialist Party. But a rump PSP still
continued. Then again the SSP and the PSP merged to form
the Socialist Party. But this unity was short-lived too. A group
again split up to form the SSP. Later this group joined an
alliance of the rightist parties to form the Bhartiya Lok Dal.
An enfeebled Socialist Party continued its uneventful existence
till after the Emergency when it finally merged with the
Bhartiya Lok Dal, the Cong (O) and the Jana Sangh to form
the Janata Party.

The unity efforts and splits moving in quick succession
reflected the conflict of two opposite motivations operating at
the same time: unity moves resulted from the compulsions of
power; disunity from the conflict of policies and personalities, the
latter also to some extent reflecting the different styles of political action. As through the years the mass base of these parties
had been whittled away there was not much to hold them back
from decisions either way. They did not have much to lose
from these moves as they were no more anchored to definite
classes of people by their commitment to certain social goals.

One effect of the flight from the masses was that the
irrational appeal based on caste, community, religion or region
grew in importance. To garner the forces represented by them
one did not have to go in for grass-root work. Their response
is automatic, unconcerned with material gain or loss. Through
all the ups and downs of India's politics the parties which
sustained their appeal were the Jana Sangh, the DMK or the
ADMK, the Akalis, and that section of the BLD which owed
loyalty to Mr Charan Singh.

But the appeals of these groups were either irrelevant to the
real problems of the people or ran counter to them. In any
case they did not add up to a serious challenge to the Congress.
The Congress all along had one advantage. Having the government in hand it could ladle out benefits at various levels and
this was enough to keep the Congressmen occupied at the

different tiers of its organisational hierachy down to the village. It also created a certain kind of grass-root contact even though of a perverse nature. In times of elections a huge army of the direct beneficiaries of its power could be mobilised to muster or manipulate votes in its favour.

Owing to the above-mentioned factors the authority of the Congress government superficially appeared stable since there was no direct challenge to it. But in reality the only stabilising factor was its hold over power. Underneath, the vast majority of the people seethed with discontent. Eruption of mass protests, sometimes taking the form of insurgency, was quite frequent. But lacking a common focus or an organising centre these protests would either die away of their own accord or were ruthlessly put down if they posed a real threat. The response of the opposition parties to these protests followed a predictable pattern. They would like to use these protests to bolster up their own election prospects, but they would not seriously try to find a solution to the basic issues which led to these protests. Perhaps because even the opposition wanted those basic issues to be swept under the carpet.

The Communist Party, with its commitment to work for the poorest and its ideological dedication, could have become the most powerful mass force in the conditions of India. But apart from the common factor of the origin of its leadership it suffered also from its external connections and its anti-democratic dogma. When it worked among the people, it won a strong and abiding influence. But owing to quirks of events in the international field it would make sudden turn-abouts in its policies (as in 1942 during the Quit India Movement or in 1948 when it fell in line with the ultra-revolutionary line of the Cominform) and destroy its base or isolate itself from the masses in the process.

Besides, ideology alone is not enough to sustain a man in his revolutionary ardour for a lifetime unless it also somehow conforms to his social ethos. And this cannot completely be abstracted from the social background of the person. To a communist member belonging to the elite, work among the masses could be a political duty, but only with great strain could it be his whole life (saints excepted, of course). He has to have life also outside the narrow compass of his political duties and even narrower routine of the social life of men among whom he has to work. The liberation of the people could also mean for him a liberation of the self from the mean life in the midst of the people, He naturally would like the revolution quick. Theoretically, a revolution could be a matter of generations. But personally he would be impatient of delays; he would like the revolution made to order and on schedule. Since history or revolution does not respect personal preferences and follows a schedule all its own, there would be frustration at the slow pace of events. This inevitably led the communist leaders to the affirmation of the communist dogma that the democratic-parliamentary process was a bourgeois trap to strangle the revolutionary upsurge of the people. But often there was no upsurge in fact. So a section of the communists tried often to invent one. This was the extremist reaction. Even when the communist leaders were compelled by events to work in the parliamentary institutions they never got over their impatience and the resulting antipathy to these. So even while working the system they would disavow any intention to carry the game indefinitely. All this to them was merely an interim arrangement till the final hour arrived. This created a lack of credibility about their democratic professions among the people and a lack of zeal among the rank and file to put their entire energy unreservedly in the organisation of the party for parliamentary work.*

This contradiction is basic to the many splits in the Indian communist movement. Faced with the above condition some of its members took the bit in the teeth and plunged into political pyrotechnics. Others have uneasily balanced their denunciation of parliamentarism with participation in parliamentary work. A third group, while paying lip-service to revolutionary conviction like members of other political parties, has sought accommodation in the constitutional parliamentary framework. However, on the whole their professions have

---

* It was in the face of a similar dilemma that the Italian, the French and the Spanish communist parties have come out with open avowal of faith in pluralist democracy—a new faith, Eurocommunism.

injected a sense of doubt about the efficacy and viability of the democratic system.

The Sarvodaya leaders have added their own bit to under-mine the democratic political system. They spared no efforts to convince the world that politics is a dirty thing and that decent people should keep clear of it. They themselves, of course, never repudiated those privileges and support that accrued to them through the political agencies. As it was, people were already getting disillusioned with the political system to deliver the goods. But this kind of pontification by men who were considered above the common run of men made them further apathetic to politics. This always proved advantageous to the ruling party which had other means to approach the people. At this juncture to generalise the guilt of polititicians tended to minimise the guilt of those who held power and who alone could use it for good or evil.

The foregoing discussion of the role of the elite in our politics should not lead to the conclusion that others than those belonging to the elite were completely excluded from a political role. In a vast country like India the various elected bodies, right from the Panchayat to the Lok Sabha, could not all be manned with members of the privileged elite. So a large number of men coming from the lower orders did inevitably get into the political system. The process of elections also saw to it that a few men from these orders from the villages got even into the upper reaches of the parliamentary system. In the normal course this should have democratised the whole system through promoting a greater degree of vertical mobility. However, certain factors worked as barriers to this development. In the first place, the democratic organs at the lower levels such as the Panchayats and the Municipalities had few powers, were often at the mercy of the bureaucrats and the higher governmental bodies which could at will supersede them. This discouraged men of ability and integrity from participating in them. They did not see much hope of making effective use of them. The result was that these bodies turned into little dens of corruption where men with petty ambition sought to enrich themselves on the scarce resources of these bodies. So they did not work as recruiting centres for cadres for higher political responsibility.

Still a few men did rise from mean beginnings into higher legislative and executive bodies. But in almost all cases they were dazed by the pomp of these bodies. They tried to adapt themselves to the new environment, adopted the life-style of the elite and in the process got alienated from their own people. They developed the illusion that they themselves were possessed of some superior quality which raised them to their new position. The whole paraphernalia of the office with its system of attention and obsequiousness, and the glare of publicity made these men forget their social root. They began soon to be ashamed of their origin and tried to cover it. They turned into comic figures as they sought to be a deity to the members of their own class. Their whole fire was exhausted in trying pathetically to look similar to the elite and superior to their own fellowmen. And finally they ended by taking sides with men against whom they should have been fighting.

Lacking roots among the people and lacking any serious intention to work for the people politics inevitably became a game of empty gestures without any clear-cut objective except somehow to acquire and hold power. When objectives are ill-defined or murky then there is a temptation to personalise politics. Political battles are often fought around symbols. But these symbols often concretise a complex of attitudes to real problems. Where such problems remain undefined the symbols point to vague abstractions. The personality of Mrs Gandhi became such a symbol signifying vague aspirations to some and anathema to others. Her chief strength lay in projecting herself as the saviour of the poor through a series of clever manoeuvres and catchy slogans after the split in the Congress in 1969. It cost her nothing in terms of real concessions to the poor.

For a while the strategy worked well. She was able to humble her opponents, and emerged as the unchallenged master of the situation after the Lok Sabha and Vidhan Sabha polls of 1971 and 1972 respectively. She got a two-thirds majority in the Lok Sabha and comfortable majorities in most of the States. She was poised, if she wanted, to bring about any kind of revolutionary change in the socio-economic field. But she did practically nothing.

Slogans can win only temporary laurels. They are not solutions of concrete problems. So while the walls were being plastered with slogans eulogising her great achievements, the basic economic issues kept fermenting underneath. Sooner or later she had to settle account with these issues. The year 1974 faced her with the choice of her life. She had either to abjure the path of surface manoeuvres and settle down to the real problem of changing society or curb people's aspirations (she herself had raised) using in full measure the new power she had acquired.

Chapter Four

The Clamp Down

I

The Indian political system which rests on a small elite has as a consequence of this fact a narrow and fragile economic base. Even a minor setback in an important sector of production or a bottleneck in distribution tends to throw this system in turmoil. Besides, the low rate of growth has left a large and growing army of the unemployed whose frustration and anger are quick to reach a flash point. It is especially so with the educated unemployed and the students who are faced with an uncertain future.

The stagnation of the economy was turning to a critical point by the year 1974. On 9 January 1975, B.M. Bhatia wrote in the *The Statesmen*:

In 1974, as a result of the cumulative impact of shortages and bottlenecks in a few important sectors (steel, non-ferrous metals, coal, petroleum products, power and transport), the downward trend continued. The production of cement, for example, fell to 11.2 million tonnes in the first 10 months of 1974 compared to 12.3 million tonnes in the corresponding period of 1973 and 12.8 million tonnes in that of 1972. Data for other industries are available only for the first eight months of 1974. During this period production of mill-made cloth fell to 2,712 million metres compared to 2,753 and 2,832 million metres respectively in the corresponding periods of 1973 and 1972; jute textile to 589,000 tonnes compared to 685,700 tonnes and 758,800 tonnes respectively in the corresponding periods of 1973 and 1972; and vanaspati to 230,000 tonnes compared to 283,000 and 395,000 tonnes respectively in the corresponding periods of 1973 and 1972.

This situation in the industrial sector was coupled with drought and a bad harvest.

The period was also marked by a sharp rise in prices. Quoting the Reserve Bank's report on Currency and Finance, *The Statesman* of 16 December 1974 reported:

The price index was 198.8 two years ago (June 1972). It advanced by 42.7 points to 241.5 in June 1973 and further galloped by 67.4 points to 308.9 in June 1974, recording an expansion of 55% in the course of two years—on an average 2.3% per month. There had not been any respite since then. The index had reached 319.8 by 16 October 1974.

According to the same report there had been a sharp rise in the number of educated unemployed—from 2.6 million in 1972-73 to 3.5 million in 1973-74.

There had also been a gradual decline in the per capita consumption of such essential items as food grains which between 1955 and 1975 had declined from 430 gms per day to 415.3 gms per day and cloth from 14.4 metres to 12.9 metres. As inequality grew the number of those living below poverty line increased by nearly 50 per cent between 1960 and the middle of the 70's. A democratic system is liable to buckle under such strain.

There were acute shortages of food grains and various other essential commodities as the year 1974 ensued. This as usual led to public agitations. But the Congress Party and its leader, Mrs Indira Gandhi, flushed with the unprecedented victory at the polls responded with force. First in Gujarat and then in the spring of 1974 in Bihar the agitation of the students for cheaper food and other basic articles, in the face of repression, took on political overtones. Now the repressive measures of the goverment began to be related to certain basic faults of the electoral system and political corruption, which had for some time become matters of strident public debate. There followed a demand for the dissolution of Assemblies and re-election under reformed electoral laws. In Gujarat owing largely to factional reasons Mrs Gandhi had the Assembly dissolved when Mr Morarji Desai undertook a fast to press this demand. Bihar was chosen as an arena where the masses had to be taught to behave. So the dissolution demand along with the rest was turned down. The agitation gained momentum and reached dimensions much beyond what had been attained even during the Quit India movement. Around a hundred thousand BSF and CRP men were posted to assist the State administration. Arrests, lathi charge and even shooting became the order of the day. The people of the State were put virtually under a state of siege. But nothing seemed to avail against the mass upsurge. Thus a stalemate between the state power and the people's power continued.

In Gujarat fresh elections were held under pressure from Mr Morarji Desai who again undertook an indefinite fast on the issue. The results of Gujarat elections were disturbing to Mrs Gandhi. The Congress was reduced to a minority whereas it held a comfortable majority before. Assembly elections in Uttar Pradesh held a little while earlier had also shown a big decline in Congress support. These were disturbing trends.

Mr Jayaprakash Narayan, who since April 1974 had taken a leading hand in the Bihar movement, made the dissolution of the Bihar Assembly a prestige issue. When Mrs Gandhi proved obdurate he sought to spread the agitation to other States. The massive turn-out in his meetings, even though failed to generate a Bihar type mass movement, indicated that in the country there was a growing restivencess against the Congress which at the time had a brute majority in the Lok Sabha. But Mrs Gandhi thought she could weather the storm as the elections were still remote. In any case she had no intention of going for a mid-term poll in response to the agitations.

The future could not but worry her. She could not hope

to coast along for all time on her past popularity. She had already shot her populist bolt in 1972 when she gave her *Garibi-Hatao* slogan. Now the populist wind was blowing against her. There was now only one way to win back the masses: that is, by translating slogans into solid acts. But her whole milieu militated against such a course. She had in the past few years accumulated unprecedented power and position. But these had been achieved, as it always happens, by gathering a coterie consisting of the capitalists who had placed at her disposal their purse and within certain limits their Press, and an army of tub-thumping and conspiring sycophants who had been promoted to the high offices of the state and the party. All the members belonging to this coterie had their own axes to grind. Besides, the entire elitist outfit of the administration was anti-democratic and opposed to a radical change. And she had to take them along. Without them she could be nothing as she was as much their creation as they were her's. They shut her off from the people and knowledge of the real condition in the country. Instead she was kept in a make-believe world of comforting illusions of progress and prosperity. Her ignorance of reality was appalling. In the midst of acute distress she spoke in public meetings of great prosperity she found around.

It is a sacrosanct belief among the privileged that agitations are not responses to some genuinely felt need but the work of meddlesome agitators. So the agitations could be easily dismissed. In response to the popular agitation the usual talk in these circles was that the root cause of all trouble lay in excessive democracy. A Congress MP belonging to the Socialist Forum, Mr Shashi Bhushan, even gave a call for a limited dictatorship under Mrs Gandhi. Silencing the people appeared the most appropriate way to serenely solve the many economic problems of the country. Mr Ramesh Thapar in the *Political and Economic Weekly* of 25 January 1975 proposed postponement of the Lok Sabha election for two years so that economic measures to overcome economic crisis could be implemented. This was the climate of opinion emanating from the knowledgeable people in which she had to operate.

She had acquired power. But to retain that power she had

to remain a prisoner of the vested interests and the forces she had fostered round her. And they closed to her the other path to power that lies in efforts to gain the genuine support of the people: through dedication to their cause. That entailed willingness to abdicate power if people so wished, i.e., the wholehearted acceptance of the democratic credo.

The path of power she had chosen, the only path of power open to those who in the context of Indian poverty hope to tread without hurting the susceptibilities of the privileged, led to one destination: some kind of authoritarianism. She had already forged the instrument of a police state with the expansion of the intelligence network to keep a watchful eye on the activities of the citizens, the politicians and even her own cabinet colleagues. Every kind of intelligence was placed directly under her.

The officialdom with the tradition to which it was heir always looked at dissidence, debate and demonstration as so much nuisance. It was all along working from the shadows in the same direction. It not only exceeded its authority when dealing with mass disorders but was liberal with suggestions to end them in the only way it knew: through terror. Over six months before 26 June 1975 they had come out with the suggestion of imposing internal Emergency to control possible disturbances when the idea of arresting Mr Jayaprakash Narayan was first mooted. That was when the Bihar movement was at its peak. C.S. Pandit reports:

The consensus in the high-powered committee of Central Police and Intelligence chiefs was that it would lead to widespread unrest and violence in the country. However, it was at a meeting of this committee that the chiefs of the Intelligence Bureau and the Central Bureau of Investigation at that time suggested that all that reaction could be prevented through a clamp down of full emergency powers all over the country. They singled out the press and the mass media for total control. In fact, the chiefs of the IB and the CBI were then asked to prepare contingency plans in case it was felt necessary to put their suggestions into operation at short notice.[1]

So her own preference and the circumstances of her hold over power were moving her in the direction of authoritarian rule. The Allahabad High Court verdict of 12 June 1975, setting aside her election to the Lok Sabha and disqualifying her for six years from contesting any election accelerated the march to her inexorable destiny.

The leaders of the opposition parties comprising the Cong (O), the Jana Sangh, the BLD, and the Socialist Party saw in the verdict their opportunity to dislodge Mrs Gandhi from power as a prelude to cut the Congress to size. Since the split in the Congress in 1969 Mrs Gandhi had emerged as the undisputed leader of the Congress. Since 1971 she had humbled all the leaders of her party to the status of obedient minions. Without her the Congress would be leaderless. Many of the leaders so reduced were not too happy with Mrs Gandhi. The leaders of the opposition even hoped to make a common cause with some of them once the watching eye of the Big Sister was absent. The opposition, which was as much cut off from the people as the ruling party, could not hope for a better opportunity. That would obviate the need for mass involvement. They had so far relied entirely on Mr Jayaprakash Narayan for mass appeal. But they could not be sure how long this sudden access to popularity would last. Mr Jayaprakash Narayan had no mass organisation nor had he any concrete programme beyond a proclamation of noble intentions. The chief support of his movement came from the educated youth. There was no doubt about their enthusiasm. But lacking any clear perception of the problems the nation faced and their solution, the youth movement could prove merely froth on the surface. So the opposition set about making the most of this opportunity.

Demand was voiced from various platforms for Mrs Gandhi's resignation. But Mrs Gandhi was unwilling to oblige. True to their character, the leaders of the opposition rather than

[1]C.S. Pandit, *End of An Era: The Rise and Fall of Indira Gandhi* Allied Publishers, Delhi, 1977, p-7

taking the issue to the people for mass mobilisation chose tamely to stage a *dharna* before the Rashtrapati Bhavan. However, feelings ran high throughout the country. The demand might snowball. So Mrs Gandhi took the offensive. She had in the past few years acquired the technique of mass mobilisation through the use of official machinery. Her managers ran hotfoot to gather the tongawallas, mobilised the Delhi Transport Corporation employees who rushed to Mrs Gandhi's residence with buses packed with hired demonstrators from the neighbouring industrial areas and slums, and collected a medley of other supporters. Thus an assortment of crowds kept coming to her place for days voicing their confidence in her and their denunciation of the judiciary and the Allahabad High Court judge for their alleged complicity with the CIA. Even the effigy of the judge was burnt before her house.

It became obvious that Mrs Gandhi was preparing to strike. It was only then that the opposition leaders woke up to the need for some kind of a mass agitation. A committee was formed to organise a peaceful agitation to force Mrs Gandhi to respect the verdict of the court and to step down till the Supreme Court gave its judgment in which she had preferred an appeal. It was to make public this decision that the historic Ramlila Ground meeting was held on 24 June 1975, which among others was addressed by Mr Jayaprakash Narayan. People sat through the meeting in heavy downpour. It was obvious that mass response would not be wanting for the proposed agitation. In the latter part of his speech in this meeting Mr Jayaprakash Narayan made the rather innocuous appeal to the police and the army personnel not to obey illegal orders. In support of his appeal he also quoted the relevant section of the police code.

Something meanwhile was brewing up in the Congress camp itself. A large number of MPs felt that Mrs Gandhi should make way for one of her colleagues to take up the leadership of the party till she was cleared by the Supreme Court. None of them, however, suggested a lack of confidence in her as their leader. It was suggested only as an interim arrangement to meet the demands of propriety.

But Mrs Gandhi was not sure of the outcome of the Court

hearing. She was even less sure about the loyalty of her colleagues. It remains one of the weaknesses of personalised politics that the loyalty of men wavers with the turn in the political fortune of the leader. And Mrs Gandhi, who had in the
past considered her allies expendable at her earliest convenience, had even less reason to trust any one of them. She might
have genuine fear that any one getting into the prime ministership would develop a vested interest in her ouster from politics.
She alone, therefore, could organise her salvage operation
from the vantage point of her premiership. And so the die
was cast.

Every dictator needs a grandiose purpose as an excuse to
impose his or her dictatorship. And Mrs Gandhi too had to
find one. So it was announced that there was a deep-laid conspiracy to undermine the democratic system in the country. It
was also alleged, indirectly hinting at Mr Jayaprakash Narayan's
call to the police and the armed forces, that attempts were
made to spread disaffection in the armed forces. It was further
insinuated that there was an attempt at destabilisation and a
parallel with Chile was drawn obviously to indicate links with
a foreign Power. Plots of large-scale violence and disruption
too were alleged. So the imposition of Internal Emergency on
26 June 1975, just thirteen days after the Allahabad High
Court judgment unseating Mrs Gandhi, was acclaimed by her
supporters and the Communist Party of India as a timely
move to save democracy and the integrity of the nation from
the forces of disruption.

Whatever the immediate reason, Mrs Gandhi quickly moved
to settle account with the forces which had plagued her in the
past and could prove future irritants. Opposition leaders
naturally were the first victims. All of those on whom the
government could lay hands were arrested. Warrants of arrest
were issued against most others. The students and their institutions received the closest attention of the police. The students
being more sensitive had provided the bulk of the activists of
the Naxalite movement and had been also the backbone of
the Gujarat and the Bihar movements. All such students and
teachers who in the eye of the government were politically
active or inclined to oppose the government were taken into

custody. Strong police pickets were placed around colleges and universities. Through a system of checks an attempt was also made in educational institutions to insulate the students from contacts with outsiders. Campuses of educational institutions were infested with plain-clothed policemen and spies. Then started a process of brainwashing not only through normal propaganda channels, but also by introducing political issues in the courses of study and examination papers of school children, who were expected to write in support of Mrs Gandhi and the Emergency.

To cut people off completely from every source of information a strict censorship was imposed. Newspapers and news agencies had to submit to pre-censorship. To make the censorship more effective at the source where news is gathered the different news agencies were amalgamated in one agency, Samachar, which was put effectively under government control.

A major source of disaffection could be the intelligentsia which had been quite vociferous in the past. It had the greatest stake in free institutions and the freedom of expression. So it came in for special attack. It was alleged that freedom of expression so far had been enjoyed only by these handful of people, which of course was a fact. But it was not inferred or argued from this that the freedom of expression be extended to make it available to all. No, not at all. Rather it was thought that this freedom be denied uniformly to all. The only freedom of expression now allowed was of approval of everything that the government did.

Many thought that the newspapermen and a majority of the intelligentsia, the teachers, the lawyers, the poets, the writers and the artists, who often joined wordy crusades for freedom of the people in distant lands—often against Yankee Imperialism and at other times against communist subversion of free institutions—would in a body resist the onslaught against their own freedom. But nothing of the kind happened. Barring a handful of men the entire intelligentsia knuckled under. A large number of senior editors behaved like chastened schoolboys before Mrs Gandhi and promised to impose self-censorship, which promise they faithfully kept. Others had a sudden change of heart and began to find every kind of virtues in Mrs Gandhi, where they had found none in the past.

And suddenly a new star was discovered in the political firmament, Sanjay Gandhi. The newspapers and magazines would vie with each other to display his photograph on the cover page or other prominent places of their periodicals and papers, and carry copious stories about his great exploits. The intellectuals would invite him to address them and would come "amazed" at his knowledge and wisdom. Authors would write lyrical biographies of 'this greatest youth genius' of the world.

Had a magic transformation taken place in the minds of the men? Or, were these men intimidated by the terror let loose by the government? In fact, there was no magic. Terror of course there was, but not of the magnitude as to cause such a sudden and shameful volte-face. Not many editors and men of letters were arrested and none subjected to the kind of torture to which their opposite numbers in some other authoritarian regimes, or some political workers and youth in India itself, had been subjected. But the intelligentsia was beaten by its own contradiction arising from its privileged position. It had no doubt concern for its freedom, as it was an essential ingredient of its self-regard. But it could not also conceive itself in a role where it was divested of its position and privileges which marked it off from the rest of the people. Assertion of freedom could mean loss of job, could mean even prison, deprivation of many comforts to the family to which it might be used, or, in some cases even destitution. Both the alternatives faced it with a loss of self-esteem. In the first case, however, it was notional affecting a person only emotionally, perhaps lowering him in the eyes of his peers. But in the second case the loss was more tangible and left him with an uncertain future. So the surrender of freedom appeared the better course to save his situation.

From this came a gradual abdication of responsibility. So long as freedom was assured the intelligentsia always claimed for itself a major share in shaping the policies of the nation. The intellectuals and the newepapermen from their high perches showered the politicians with elaborate advice as to

what was good to them and to the nation. The unlettered
politician, it was thought, needed guidance from the men who
really had the inside knowledge. Suddenly it began to appear
that politics was none of their direct concern. They were in
the job as newspapermen, university teachers or research
workers and had to carry on their jobs as best as the situation
permitted. And they could not be held responsible for what
was beyond their control. Then they began to be more objective, tried to balance the pros and cons of the Emergency.
Certain features of the Emergency, they argued, were no doubt
regrettable, but then its positive achievements could not be
denied. And as time passed, and the government's Public
Relations Office began to play a more positive role in furnish-
ing information, the balance began to tilt in favour of the gains
of the Emergency. Its loss, the loss of freedom, remained only
a backdrop which began slowly to fade in the memory as the
routine of the comfortable life and the new engagements began
to make their claims on the time and the mind of the nation's
think tank.

But initially the acceptance of or support to the Emergency
was shamefaced and reluctant. But soon that class of the elite,
which is entirely a product of the post-independence era, began
to take a hand. This is a class which has flourished under
political patronage, and finds nothing—servility, bribery or
betrayal—degrading as long as it could promote its self-
interest. So immediately after the Emergency some intellectuals
began to pay visits to Mrs Gandhi to assure her of their
support. Others felt encouraged. After their initial hesitation
more of the editors and intellectuals took this positive step.
Finally, not to be upstaged, the rest of them followed suit, and
the trickle of men turned into a regular stream of visitors
representing the cream of Indian society. They waited long
hours to have the great lady's *Darshan*, to snivel before her,
to swear fealty to her and finally convinced her that they were
men fit to be trampled under. So her attack on the intelligentsia grew in vigour.

The working class in the organised sector of industries also
surrendered without a fight although it too had a great stake
in a liberal democratic order—in fact, more than any other

class. Loss of freedom to it meant that it lost the right of collective bargaining. It could not exercise such of its legitimate trade union rights, as of strike, demonstration, picketing, etc., which in the ultimate analysis are the only effective means to get its grievances redressed. But just as the intelligentsia surrendered its freedom due largely to its concern for its status, the workers gave way due to a fear of loss of job. And in the Indian context this fear was enough to beat them.

The standard of life enjoyed by workers in the organised sector is far superior to that of a vast majority of even the small property owners in the village, not to speak of the standard of living of the marginal farmers and the landless agricultural workers. Compared to the latter they certainly are a privileged lot. In a country with a large unemployed population which is subjected to a subhuman existence and where opportunity for alternative employment in industry once a job is lost is non-existent, losing a job is among the most horrifying prospects before a worker. And during the Emergency it became plain that any protest would amount to arrest and, worse still, the loss of job. Most workers have relatives who themselves are poor and could not be looked to for support in times of need. So opposition to the Emergency might even mean abandoning the family to starvation.

Even then if the workers were assured of a reasonable chance of success or even a major struggle, they could have attempted some form of resistance. But as the situation obtained they were badly divided. The Indian National Trade Union Congress and the All-India Trade Union Congress, the two major trade union organisations, were tied to the apron strings of Mrs Gandhi and were hailing the Emergency as a pre-emptive attack against fascism. They were sure to act as strike breakers in the event of any industrial action. With such division it would have been suicidal for the remaining organisations to give call for a major action. In any event not many even among the other leaders of the trade unions were clear as to what was happening. They were simply stunned into inaction.

But this state of the trade union leadership was not entirely fortuitous. This arose in the kind of development the unions had. Initially, there indeed had been some militant trade union movement when they were getting organised. But later with the growing ability of industry in certain sectors to pay comparatively good wages, militant action was replaced by negotiated settlements. Labour legislations also made strikes difficult and helped to make industrial tribunals, arbitrations and conciliation machinery for all practical purposes the only means to wrest concessions from the employers. A very important feature of this development was that trade unions thrived less on initiating a demand and fighting for it through strikes and more on pressurising the government to appoint commissions, or pass legislation on these demands, whose findings and provisions they would try to get implemented mostly through negotiations or legal channels. In this process the trade unions got closely enmeshed with the government departments. They were characterised by a leadership which comprised shrewd negotiators and legal experts rather than militant agitators. There were exceptions, no doubt, but this was the broad profile of the trade union leadership. It was little suited to a struggle which had to be illegal and in direct confrontation with the government.

It was a depressing spectacle to find trade unions coming out openly in support of the Emergency and its stringent measures which rendered their own existence untenable. However, this kotowing before authority went on till the end of the Emergency. But this effort to please and placate did not bring the workers any gain. They found on the other hand their statutory bonus taken away, Compulsory Deposit Scheme imposed and had even to face large-scale retrenchment against which they had no means to protest.

In the beginning the people in the unorganised sectors of the economy whose dealings with the government are indirect and whose concern for public affairs minimal or non-existent were left off lightly. Thus the self-employed, the small trader, and the overwhelming part of our population, the rural people, did not feel affected by what had happened. They rarely expressed their opinion about political affairs. In any case no one had bothered about what happened to them or listened to what they had to say. They certainly were surprised to learn about the arrest of the leaders and were also pained if they respected some of the arrested leaders. But politics was something beyond them. So they did not worry much. Thus the only part of the population whose reaction or resistance could have been a matter of concern—no police force could have coped with the resistance spread in five hundred thousand villages—remained aloof. Mrs Gandhi even took care to announce certain measures in her much touted twenty-point programme to bring some benefits to the poorest in the villages who have been a permanent source of rural discontent. So, for the time being the Emergency appeared to have rendered Mrs Gandhi invulnerable to any political pressure or agitation.

Now with her two-thirds majority in the Lok Sabha, whose most vocal members opposed to her were safely locked up, and proceedings of Parliament barred to public through strict censorship on their publication, she was free to do what she liked with the law and the constitution and to render judicial process topsyturvy to ensure the reversal of the Allahabad High Court judgment in her election case. But by the time the election laws were changed and a favourable verdict obtained for Mrs Gandhi in the Supreme Court, this case had ceased to interest any one. By that time a new political system had come to stay in India for which the law and the constitution were merely a disguise. Now all law and authority flowed from Mrs Gandhi and a small coterie surrounding her. But perhaps that too only ostensibly and at the highest level where major political decisions were taken. For the rest the decision lay with the bureaucratic apparatus which suddenly came into its own. The vast bureaucracy which always nursed its old contempt for the people and popular authority found its finest hour. It suddenly revived.

The administrative bureaucracy and the police (which had never been revamped to suit the democratic system) under the Emergency were unleashed on the people. They had always chafed under the restraints placed by the legislatures which seemed unduly to interfere in their domain. They had equally been peeved by the judicial restraints placed on their action. All this appeared unnecessarily to complicate the simple job of keeping people on the right track. Now it appeared that the bureaucratic bailiwicks would be free from the intrusions of the political busy-bodies. Similarly, the police could now have a free hand in handing out summary justice without the fear of being answerable to any one. The rule of the baton and the bullet was assured. They could not only set political matters right but also settle a few scores of their own as Emergency bonus. They after all were now the chief bulwark of the political system and they surely had to have reward for the extra responsibility thrust on their shoulders. There were of course notable exceptions. But their number was small and hence they could not make any impact on the general run of the services of which they were part. (It is extremely naive to blame the large number of murders and tortures in police custody on Mrs Gandhi and Sanjay Gandhi. Local administration was directly responsible for most of them. Mrs Gandhi of course is responsible indirectly for bringing into existence a system which must thrive on the criminal propensities of the law enforcement authority.)

As the authority passed into the hands of the bureaucracy and the police the impact of the Emergency began to be felt far and wide. Whereas repression and atrocities in the beginning were selective, now they tended to be more general. Authority of the magistracy and police is ubiquitous in this country and they could not help exuding the newly-acquired power. Soon people even in the remotest village began to have a taste of the new political system. Now even a normal administrative work would not proceed without the coercive imprint of the Emergency. This became evident in the method of food procurement in villages, tax and loan collection, in the way 'unauthorised' houses and hutments were demolished and above all in the family planning drive. The many excesses which have been recounted after the Emergency were largely a product of this zeal.

This is not to say that the responsibility for the excesses lay only with those who administered the measures under the Emergency and not with the chief author of the dispensation. Dictatorship is a method of administration, which by its very nature transcends the limits of law and morality. Dictators

place themselves beyond law and morals. And if they themselves are beyond law how their limbs that administer their
realm could be stayed or limited by law. So an element of
arbitrariness at every level is an essential ingredient of dictatorship. The chief instrument of dictatorship is terror. And people
can be terrorised only when the blow on them falls inexplicably
and unexpectedly—that is, in an arbitrary manner. The moment
limitations are set by law, morals or custom, the administrative action could be anticipated, remedies devised and the
element of terror minimised. So no dictatorship can be benign
or benevolent. It has to rest on the shoulders of little dictators,
each of whom has his own axe to grind, and invariably at the
cost of the people.

Those who think that the excesses were unintended and were
a few obtrusive features of the Emergency are, therefore,
mistaken. The excesses were its essential features. It is through
such acts that a dictatorship proclaims to the people the
omnipotence of its power over their lives and property.

II

People generally agree that there were rigours and hardships
during the Emergency. But many would also point to the
undeniable gains (the radio and the newspapers all talked of
them). Some of these supposed gains were minor, the other
major ones. In the first category came such gains as the movement of trains on time and queueing up for buses in the capital,
and the cleanliness which it was pointed out was becoming very
much evident in the cities. Among the major gains that were
pointed out were the highly improved industrial relations, price
stability, impressive spurt in the export of such non-traditional
items as steel and engineering goods, and record output and
procurement of food grains.

Whatever its worth as a justification for dictatorship, even
factually the timely running of trains was a wholly exaggerated
claim. As much of the Emergency face-lifting was a publicity
exercise, some order certainly was brought about on the
trunk services and the long-distance trains, since they
touched large cities and could easily impress foreigners and

publicity men who count. But the short-distance trains and the railway services in the backyards remained much as before. Even the punctuality of the long-distance trains was less than perfect. It was not unusual to find even some of these trains running hours behind schedule. But when this happened there was no one around to point out. No newspaper dared publish such reports.

It is the same story about the discipline of the Delhi commuters. Of course one does not need an Emergency to enforce the queueing habit. People of Bombay or Bangalore had acquired that civilised habit long before any one had heard about an Emergency rule. But the unruly behaviour of the Delhi commuter is a reflection of the general political and social ethos of this capital of India. It reflects the Delhi elite's ambition to pre-empt position and power disregarding the claims or convenience of others. That Mr Sanjay Gandhi could become the idol of the Delhi youth even before the Emergency could have its impact felt was largely a manifestation of this singular ethos of the city. What made him this idol was his unwillingness to measure his merit against that of others and his impatience to wait for his turn. No civic decency can bear the burden of such imperiousness. The Emergency could not improve the matter either. At a few points people did of course queue up with the active intervention of the police. It worked, for example, near the Central Secretariat where the meek *Babus* exhausted from the day's work would dumbly join the line. Similarly at a few other starting points where there was a reasonable certainty of getting a bus quickly there would be a queue. But through most of the routes people would jostle, push and pull to be the first in the bus. It may be said in extenuation of the poor commuters that they were provided with so few buses which plied with unpredictable frequency that they lost patience. But it is difficult to see how this impatience could improve matters. Any way the Emergency certainly failed to convince them.

One sphere in which the Emergency had a solid achievement was in its cleansing operation. It was understandable too. The programme fully conformed to the taste and preferences of

the elite. It was in this operation that all the repressed antagonism of the elite to the under-class of the Indian people found
its full vent. The dwellings of the poor men, their shabby
jhuggies had been a perpetual eyesore to those who lived in
their spacious bungalows and luxury flats. These not only
polluted the city but even invaded their much manicured
neighbourhoods. They needed of course the dwellers of these
jhuggies as housemaids, servants, vegetable vendors or caterers
of many other odd services. But they were impervious to the
latter's simple needs for dwellings. It was none of the former's
business to find how in a city with houses so scarce and rents
so high, these people retained at little pittances could find
houses to live in. So the whole stinking lot had to be cleared
away. And they did a thorough job of it. In Mr Sanjay
Gandhi they found a pliable tool to bring their dream of a
clean city to reality. He was egged on with high praises of
his beautification scheme.

Hoardings at important places urged people to keep 'Delhi
the City of Smiles' clean. And the bulldozers became active.
The dwellings were razed to the ground, and the people from
these dwellings, six hundred thousand of them, comprising
nearly a sixth of the city's population, were carted off with
their wives, baggages and babies to different destinations several
miles away from the city, to the mosquito-infested marshes of
Khichripur, Jehangirpuri and similar other places where one
could not get even drinking water. In this way the city of
smiles got rid of its lachrymal lot.

No one dared raise a voice. Resistance was out of the question. The operation was backed with all the majesty and *force
majeure* of the newly-created state power. Turkman Gate
formed a solitary exception. There, in the face of the twin
operation, that is, operation demolition and operation sterilisation, a voice of defiance was raised. When the police tried to
bludgeon the people into submission, the latter met physical
force with physical force. Then a massacre followed the like of
which many people alleged Delhi had not witnessed since the days
of Nadir Shah. Unarmed men, women and children were
beaten, bayoneted and shot on the roads and inside their houses.
A curfew was imposed on a large area surrounding Turkman

Gate. It continued for several days. There was a total blackout of all news. Officially, people learnt about it only when a few days later a short explanatory note condemning the people for their violence appeared in the newspapers.

Delhi was not the only city which was cleansed. Other cities and small towns too had caught this fever, though the operation was not equally neat everywhere.

Coming to the major gains, one has to concede that there was a marked improvement in industrial relations as far as strikes and agitations were concerned. The reason was not far to seek. With MISA and DIR hanging overhead there was little likelihood of trade union leaders planning strike action, though some wild-cat strikes did take place. Whatever the provocation from the side of the management, the workers could only appeal to the sense of equity of the government, a sense, incidentally, with which the government under the Emergency was not liberally endowed. So they had to swallow the humble pie and satisfy themselves with whatever a negotiated settlement could get them. It was quite natural for the spokesmen of Tatas and Birlas to feel wholly satisfied with the prevailing industrial climate, a sentiment they loudly expressed.

But these excellent industrial relations were rather asymmetrical, as their advantages lay all on one side. While the industrialists were free from strikes and agitations, the workers did not have a comparable gain. On the other hand, the industries taking advantage of the inability of the labour to agitate acted in an unrestrained way where the question of retrenching the workers or closing down industries arose. Lockouts became frequent. This situation is clearly brought out in a report published in *The Statesman* of 28 June 1977. The report, which is based on the Labour Ministry Annual Report for 1976, says :

In the public sector the total man days lost were only 0.76 million compared to 10.72 million in the private sector. While the workers demonstrated magnificent restraint some employers did not show a similar restraint which is reflected in the increase in the number of man days lost on account of lockouts. From 54% in January 1976 the percentage of time loss relating to lockouts increased to a staggering figure of 90% in May 1976.

Besides, during the Emergency several thousand units of small and medium-sized industries and several hundred units of large-scale industries shut down. House construction came almost to a halt. Thus hundreds of thousand of workers were thrown out of work. But no cognizance could be taken as there was no organised voice to draw the attention of the government or to stay the action of the employers. So the workers had silently to suffer all the agonies that came from deprivation of work. Similarly, the workers in most of the industries lost their bonus as it ceased to be statutory, and there was no way to compel the employers to pay it voluntarily.

The claims about the decline in the rate of inflation is based on a coincidence, and the impact of the Emergency was non-existent. This could be easily seen from the report published in *The Times of India* of 11 December 1975, quoting an official review :

The monthly rate of increase in the wholesale price index declined from 3 per cent in July 1974 to 2.5 per cent in August and further to 1.6 per cent in September. The wholesale price index (1961-62—100) took a downward turn after it had touched the peak of 330.7 in the third week of September 1974 and recorded a continuous decline to the first week of April 1975 when it stood at 305.9.

The annual rate of inflation (point to point comparison) which had risen to 32 per cent in September 1974 declined to 7 per cent by the first week of April 1975.

It is to be noted that the inflationary pressure had already been considerably reduced a little over two months before the proclamation of the Emergency. It has also to be recalled that around October 1974 the Bihar movement reached its peak and the agitation was getting wide support in other parts of the country. The government had been compelled under the pressure of the movement to take certain remedial measures to curb inflation which had started to have some impact.

This was made possible largely due to easing of shortages of industrial raw materials and foodgrains which were being imported on a big scale. Moreover, 1975-76 proved a year of record food production and of edible oil. All these factors helped to keep the inflationary pressure under check throughout 1975 and early part of 1976. All this had little to do with efficient management under the Emergency. Even an official survey admits as much in its report:

An analysis of wholesale prices during April-December 1975 shows that industrial raw materials (such as raw cotton and oil seeds), foodgrains and edible oils played a leading role in inducing fall in prices. By contrast, there was no significant decline in prices of intermediate products being more or less neutralised by an increase of 1.3 per cent in prices of finished products. Prices of chemicals and machinery and transport equipment showed a rising trend.[1]

So here we actually find an admission that the sectors where administrative remedies really could work (e.g. the industrial sector) remained refractory to the pressures of the Emergency. Only in the agricultural sector, where seasonal factors play a leading role or imports had temporarily pushed the prices down, there was a sizeable decline in prices.

Thus when the initial impetus of the complex of circumstances leading to the decline in the prices had been exhausted, the Emergency measures failed to bring about the much-acclaimed miracle. When the prospect for food production and oilseeds production became dim in the following year in spite of the huge stock of foodgrains in the government godowns the price began to rise once again. From March 1976 to November 1976 the prices registered a rise of 11% in eight months. The prices continued their upward trend right up to the end of the Emergency.

The record harvest of 1975-76 was more a product of the favourable monsoon than of the superior management under the Emergency. To be convinced of it one has only to look

[1]Government of India Economic Survey 1975-76, p. 16

at the harvest of the following year (i.e. 1976-77) in which not only the level of 1975-76 could not be improved but there was a sharp decline by almost ten million tonnes.

With record harvest record procurement could be expected. Since credit for food purchases by traders had been severely restricted in a year of good harvest there were few buyers in the field. The farmers had naturally to dump their product in the government godowns. In fact, the performance was repeated again in 1976-77 in a year of comparatively bad harvest. That proves nothing except the extreme vulnerability of the farming sector of the economy.

The performance in export of such items as steel and engineering goods if seen in proper perspective would appear as reflecting a dismal failure of the economy. When we think of export of steel we must bear in mind the fact that our production of saleable steel in that year was under six million tonnes in a country of almost 600 million people. England and Japan with a sixth of this population produce and use almost ten and twenty times as much steel respectively. That shows how meagre our steel production is even to keep a very modest standard of life. Why the acute shortage of steel of a year before 1975 turned suddenly into a glut should make one ponder. It could only mean one thing : industrial production and construction work in the country were coming to a standstill. This alone can explain an export of almost 1.9 million tonnes of steel out of this meagre production. A growing economy in a vast country like India should be able to absorb a much larger production. It is the same story with the engineering goods. An underdeveloped country should absorb its engineering goods for its own industrial expansion (after all much of our economy is still in the bullock-cart age). That India had to depend for their disposal on exports and joint ventures in third countries is a pathetic tale of failure, not a matter for rejoicing.

There is also another matter to be taken note of in relation to this export. India enjoys a relative advantage in the production of cheap steel owing to the availability of high-grade ore, perhaps among the best in the world, and its cheap labour. So when we sell steel to the advanced countries we allow them a great benefit. It accords well with their policy to get their semi-processed and unprocessed wares from sources where they could be produced cheaply, and use their own resources for more sophisticated products which they load on us at prices dictated by them. Such deals help maintain for them high rates of return. Would it not be much better if India used its own steel to manufacture all those things it urgently needed and it could produce? The kind of export promotion much boasted of indicated a failure or a serious misdirection of policy.

When we look closely at the claimed economic achievements of the Emergency, we find that they are largely non-existent. The simple truth is that force is no substitute for sound economic policy. It is not possible to find a police remedy for a systemic malady.

A very notable feature of the Emergency was that in order to enforce its harsh measures, Mrs Gandhi did not have to create a special organisation like the storm troopers or the Gestapo or to introduce in the administration a gang of genocidal maniacs. The existing administration was found good enough to carry out her wishes willingly. Even when there had been serious violations of law and constitution, there was no refusal. Often the administration went beyond the express orders. This revealed where the real commitment of the bureaucracy in this country lay.

Chapter Five

The Resistance

No powerful resistance against a system could be possible unless the latter became sufficiently odious in the eyes of the people. In the beginning, the meaning of the Emergency was not sufficiently clear even to the so-called politically educated. To the villagers and the poor in the cities it was one of those political changes, though somewhat of an unsual kind, which as in the past did not seem to concern them. Only to the politically committed, after the initial confusion, the meaning became clear. It was among them that the battle line was drawn.

To begin with, the opposition parties, which had been planning a national agitation on a different issue, found themselves in complete disarray. Most of their top leaders had been arrested. The few remaining, who had gone underground, were not easily to be traced. There was no co-ordination and no plan of action. A few leaders like Karpoori Thakur, who alone among the leaders had wide mass contacts, escaped to Nepal and was trying to set up an office there to conduct the movement. Nothing came of it due to the hostile attitude of the Nepal King. But his escape to Nepal created some panic even in Bihar where the activists had braved, earlier, every form of repression. They thought that matters were getting so serious that operating within the country was becoming impossible. There were others belonging to the upper classes who took the first opportunity to escape to the USA or UK, out of sheer panic no doubt, but ostensibly to conduct the fight from abroad, as if India's fight for freedom could be conducted by others and not by the people of India themselves. Many others thought there was no hope for the restoration of freedom. In the terror that ensued many deserted their parties and swore loyalty to Mrs Gandhi and her programme. Earlier, people had thought that the Jana Sangh with its cohort of RSS would be the backbone of the movement that was proposed to be launched. Now it was found that these organisations recorded the highest percentage of desertions. Many of their stalwarts, who had been arrested, tendered apologies in prison. Fortunately for them, the government was disinclined to grant pardon. So most were kept in prison till the end and their honours remained intact.

The total isolation of the political leadership from the people became evident from the fact that the arrest of all top leaders of these political parties including Jayaprakash Narayan left the nation cool. There were no spontaneous strikes, no demonstrations, no uprooting of rails. The simple fact was that the leadership of the opposition parties had failed to find their way to the hearts of the people. Their fight, though it occasionally elicited public response when it touched their problems, by and large had appeared a mere struggle for power. It took some time before people could realise that a real change in the nature of the fight had come about with the proclamation of the Emergency.

But there were sporadic acts of defiance by individuals and small groups here and there. Sometimes these touched great heights of courage. These were acts of little-known men, ordinary activists who still remain unknown or unrecognised. But altogether they could have little significance in a vast country of the size of India.

There were also isolated attempts to bring out small newssheets, handbills and appeals to people to resist the dictatorship. These were sometimes printed. But since printing was unsafe as police continued to raid the presses, mostly they were cyclostyled and then distributed or mailed. As with time the initial terror passed away and people got used to the Emergency, the number of such clandestine newsheets also grew.

The very decentralisation of these publications made it extremely difficult for the police to stamp them out of existence.
When their sources were discovered at one point and people
connected with them arrested, something would crop up
elsewhere. Mostly this work was carried on by young people.
Occasionally they showed admirable courage and ingenuity.

This kind of activity did to some extent keep people informed about some of the happenings. However, such information
was meagre. There was no organisation through which reports
and instructions could flow from all parts of the country. No
serious attempt was ever made to organise such channels of
information though the leaders who had escaped arrest did
sometimes meet. And the worst feature of it all was that
barring a handful of workers few tried to keep in close touch
with the villages where alone a sustained resistance movement
could thrive. In fact, even rural leaders left their own areas
and took shelter in far-off places, often in cities, from where they
could not even keep in touch with their own people. Thus the
bulk of the literature was circulated in the cities and in many cases
proved only of mutual benefit to the underground workers. In
Bihar owing to greater political consciousness of the people
clandestine operation was easier. The youth activists, who had
escaped arrest, did maintain regular contact with rural areas
trying to reach their literature to the villages. But there was no
clarity as to the issues on which to mobilise the peasants. So
much remained confined to general appeals to resist the
dictatorship and to providing a few bits of information that
could be gathered. In Maharashtra, circulation of literature
was more systematic and occasionally open defiance by the
Press too occurred. The journalists and men of letters in
Maharashtra showed comparatively greater courage.   •

But through nineteen months of Emergency never once was
there a serious attempt by the leaders of the parties to make a
thorough analysis of the economic and political situation so as
to discover the sources of their own failure or to find why the
nation so easily succumbed to the dictatorship. The advent of
dictatorship in some of the Western countries gave rise to a
very rich literature analysing every aspect of life, political
psychological and historical. In India these problems did not

seem to bother either the political leadership or the intellectual leaders of society. Perhaps it reflected a lack of will to continue the fight for any length of time. Or maybe there was also a sense of complicity under the apparent hostility to the system.

Whatever the reason, by early 1976 the leaders of the opposition appeared completely demoralised. A sense of despondency was visible among most of the political leaders who still were out. In this respect, however, there was a difference in the morale of those who were nearer Delhi or near the summit and those who were far off. Among those who were in the outlying areas and near the village there was less of demoralisation, and among the younger generation even a determination to carry the fight into an indefinite future. Even clandestine activities in these areas were not so clandestine. Often there could be defiance and open demonstration. However, the destiny of the movement did not lie with the latter group.

Mrs Gandhi felt quite secure in her power. Mr Jayaprakash Narayan was released when the government thought that his condition was past recovery. However, he survived. A few other leaders, who Mrs Gandhi thought were amenable to her blandishment, were released one by one. None of the leaders dared say so openly, but in subdued tones hints would be made that since now every chance of defeating Mrs Gandhi was over it would be prudent to arrive at some compromise, even though it meant operating with considerably less freedom than before the Emergency. Some men who were close to Mr Jayaprakash Narayan were even deputed to convince him of the utter hopelessness of the situation so that he might be induced to withdraw the movement which was the chief impediment to a negotiated settlement. The arrangement could have suited Mrs Gandhi perfectly as that would not only have normalised her dictatorship but even gained the acquiescence of her chief enemies. The 42nd amendment of the constitution was on the anvil formalising the extraordinary powers of the executive (it got the assent of the President on 18 December 1976). The Prevention of Publication of Objectionable Matter Act, 1976 had already been enforced since December 1975 (through an ordinance) making any criticism of the government and ministers virtually impossible. The Act could not even be challenged in a court. Any functioning of the opposition now would be within the limitations imposed by these constitutional and legal innovations. A common refrain of Mrs Gandhi's utterances in those days was that there could be no question of going back to the conditions prevailing before 26 June 1975.

While these developments were going on in the political circles, a silent change in the opposite direction was taking place in the mood of the people. This was brought about largely by the police excesses of various kinds, but in the main connected with the mass sterilisation campaign. So far the issue of political liberty had not touched the masses. But now the issue was getting concretised for them. With forced sterilisation the difference between dictatorship and democracy, between servitude and freedom became tangible.

The only kind of sterilisation that the peasant had known before was the castration of his cattle. Now when men could be caught and forcibly sterilised the implication became clear. In the eyes of the government the status of a poor man was no better than that of an animal. Thus so long as there was democracy, however poor, his status was that of a man. Now under a dictatorship he was reduced to an animal. Largely unspoken the realisation sank deep in the simple comprehension of that sleeping giant, the common mass of India. In the face of the overwhelming force of the state his resistance was mainly passive. He was forced to submit, but he submitted without condoning the act. Always a sense of humiliation and inequity was writ large on his face, it was burnt in his consciousness. Occasionally, however, this passive resistance would flare up into active one and the police were obliged to open fire and use other coercive measures to bring the masses under control. This happened at several places in Uttar Pradesh and Haryana.

Thus at the moment when the opposition leaders were despairing of any effective resistance, people were stirring into action and becoming receptive to the voice of dissent against the ruling dictatorship. This again exemplified the divorce of the political leaders from the masses. This sea change in popular mood became evident when the accused in the Baroda Dynamite case were brought for trial.

Ever since the proclamation of the Emergency Mrs Gandhi had

been talking of a deep-laid conspiracy to overthrow the government by violent means. But there was no Reichtag fire to
provide her with an evidence. Whatever resistance there was
it was so entirely peaceful and non-violent that it was difficult
for her to spot out something to show for all her accusations.
Then suddenly an occasion appeared to provide her an example.
That was the Baroda Dynamite Conspiracy in which Mr George
Fernandes had a leading hand.

The conspiracy was the result of sheer desperation of some
political leaders who were disgusted with the passivity of the
masses in general and the working class in particular. Some of
these were trade union leaders who had pinned great hopes on
the political role of the working class. But they found that the
class did not lift a finger in defence of its own rights. They had
little contact with or faith in the rural masses. So some form
of terrorism appeared the only way to rouse the masses, to
convince them that the struggle was going on. They hit on the
idea of bringing about disruption of transportation by blowing
up bridges, etc. The plan of course was childishly naive.
It was neither full-fledged terrorism which could overawe
the government nor a plan of action whose message could
be made to reach the people. Disruption of transport services
in the midst of a mass uprising to prevent mobility of the army
or their supplies is a different thing. But the kind of disruption
of train services envisaged could have been highly counter-
productive. In fact, if a train disaster had followed such a
programme then people would have turned against the per-
petrators of such action rather than the government. Fortunately,
owing to the amateurishness and lack of training of the con-
spirators the plan did not succeed. The dynamite failed to
produce the expected explosions. Soon the CBI was on their
trail and most of the people connected with this conspiracy were
arrested.

Mrs Gandhi saw in this abortive attempt her opportunity to
show to the world what she had all along been saying—the violent
nature of the conspiracy to dislodge her. She was so blinded that she
could not see that the conspiracy was posterior to the establishment of the dictatorship. It did not occur to her that once she had
clamped a brutal dictatorship under which the citizens lost even

their right to life, people would not condemn any one for daring
to destroy that dictatorship even if that entailed violent means.
She decided to make the trial of the accused a big court-
room extravaganza. With great amount of brutal torture con-
fessions were obtained from some of the accused. With months
of labour in which facts and fabrications were interwoven into
a seemingly fool-proof case the CBI produced a cart-load of
documents against the accused. Foreign Press too was allowed
in the court to make them see and tell the world what sinister
designs there were in the country.

But by this time Mrs Gandhi's credibility had gone so low,
the public opinion so completely changed that people in general
took the entire case to be a fabrication. The few who thought that
the case was real only felt admiration for the accused. Rather
than appearing criminals in their eyes they looked like heroes.
It was plain that it was not the accused but Mrs Gandhi and
her government who were on trial.

But this change of attitude was helped by two other factors
besides the family planning excesses. One was the acclimatisa-
tion to a liberal fare which imperceptibly had created among
the people a certain kind of expectation from and response
to authority. Even though laws were often violated, certain
restraints of law were expected from the authorities. That habit
of mind could not have been eradicated in a few months. It would
have needed many years of indoctrination and drilling in implicit
obedience. But Mrs Gandhi had neither the machinery nor a
coherent ideology for such an indoctrination. So as soon as the
rigours of the first few days of the Emergency relaxed, people
began to settle back in their old attitudes. Even police action
was spasmodic rather than sustained over a period. The action of
authorities was arbitrary instead of being disciplined and rigorous
in enforcing the Emergency regulations, because there was a lack
of direction or conviction. Often the police atrocities were in
response to a sudden command from above rather than as part
of a systematic pattern. Separation of powers, though not fully
developed and lately under attack, did make some headway.
Often a conflict would arise between the executive and the
judiciary. Similarly there would be a conflict between the claims
of the ruling party and the prerogatives of the administrative

bureaucracy. All this made the dictatorship a very flabby affair. So after the initial hush, criticism began to be voiced against the government though confined to close circles of friends or family.

The other factor perhaps was India's own tradition of dialogue and debate to settle the merit of an idea. Unlike many other countries, including those of the West, India never had a tradition of heresy-hunting. The social system, it is true, was often very repressive and based on great inequalities and coercion. But where ideas were concerned they were always allowed an opportunity to prevail in open debate. Even an uneducated villager in India will not accept the validity of an idea merely because it is backed by superior physical force. This addiction to logic in India has developed almost to a fault. So much so that even where an issue could be settled by examination of facts an Indian would normally insist on proving his point by arguments. To such an argumentative mind such a dramatic negation of logic as the baton of the police could not be convincing beyond a certain point.

Censorship and the suppression of free discussion made everything coming from the government source suspect. As newspaper and radio reports lost credibility, non-official news was readily believed and circulated. Even the most fantastic rumours against the government would be believed and they spread like wild fire Now public resentment took subtle forms. Jokes about the Prime Minister and her family and the stupidity of the police could be heard eveywhere. Even the school children in whom were crammed the virtues of Mrs Gandhi and her rule, out of school would have their revenge by bandying about these jokes. Thus a silent resistance was building up in the realm of comprehension and on the plane of ideas among the common people.

A dictator is rarely loved. But when from being an object of awe and reverence the dictator becomes an object of ridicule the days of the dictator are numbered.

Chapter Six

The Reprieve

In the winter of 1976 some new developments had begun to take place. A few leaders of the opposition were released. Either by accident or design those released were leaders who favoured some negotiated settlement with Mrs Gandhi. Some, like Mr Biju Patnaik, publicly expressed their admiration for the gains of the Emergency. Mr Karunanidhi, the former Chief Minister of Tamil Nadu, had worries about the enquiry instituted against him. He was playing a key role in trying to bring the various parties to the negotiating table. Mrs Gandhi of course was unyielding. In any case she did not want to create the impression that she was eager for negotiations. But she too had reasons to welcome a settlement if that could be had without any substantial concession. Lately Sanjay Gandhi had become an object of controversy in her own party, and quarters close to the communist lobby which had hitherto backed her were becoming openly critical. Mrs. Nandini Satpathy, the Orissa Chief Minister, had been forced to resign and was truculent. Mr Sidhartha Shanker Ray was in sombre mood. In Orissa and West Bengal the controversy in the party was becoming public. She knew the anti-communist bias of the opposition and perhaps hoped that they would swallow the bait if lured to save her from the communists. And there is no doubt she had the intelligence report about the prevailing demoralisation among these leaders. The leaders were extended facilities for mutual consultation. Such consultations deepened their sense of desolation. As time passed without any positive overtures or concrete proposal for negotiations from Mrs Gandhi, these leaders were steeled in their determination to surrender unconditionally. Now there was nothing to do except to work out the modalities of an honourable surrender.

But there was a snag. Those who were still in prison (and they still formed the majority) had to be consulted. Besides, the settlement had to have the blessing of Mr Jayaprakash Narayan.

On 14 December 1976 Mr. George Fernandes from prison wrote a letter to Mr N.G. Goray (who had not been arrested and represented the Socialist Party in the negotiating team) reminding him of the decision of the socialist workers' convention held some time back in Bombay, and asking him to prevent what he called a 'sell-out.'[1] He also wrote to Mr Jayaprakash Narayan informing of what was going on and his own apprehensions. Mr Jayaprakash Narayan was aware of the moves. Around the same time he addressed a letter to the leaders in Delhi who were seeking negotiations. In his letter he made it quite clear that he could not agree to any compromise unless certain basic demands restoring freedom were met. At the end of the letter he reminded them of the words of Kennedy that one should not fear to negotiate but one should not negotiate from fear. That perhaps put some shame or spunk in the leaders. After that nothing was heard of the proposed negotiations. Mrs Gandhi was interested in a surrender, not a settlement. So obviously the whole move was dropped.

There followed a lull in the situation for a while. And then in her characteristic style on 18 January 1976, Mrs Gandhi sprang a surprise by dissolving the Lok Sabha and ordering fresh elections. Why she did it remains largely a matter of speculation. Maybe she thought that the economy was taking a turn for the worse and was likely to go downhill for some

[1]See Appendices A, B and C.

more time. The prices had already begun to move up. Prospect of agricultural production was not too bright. Unemployment continued to mount. And while production in the public sector had picked up, private sector showed continued stagnation or decline. Sooner or later she had to go to the polls, since even dictators have to legitimise their rule, specially a civilian dictator. Because once the armed forces begin to feel that they are the sole prop of the dictator, their ambition to rule directly is likely to rise. So she had to seek election before the situation grew worse. And perhaps she became a victim of her own propaganda which a controlled Press and radio carried on relentlessly. With the silencing of all criticism she lacked the feedback to correct her course. She was lulled into the false belief that she enjoyed unchallenged popularity.

The other explanation offered is that the elections were hastened owing to a concern for Mr Sanjay Gandhi, who was pressing hard to be inducted early into the administration. It was stipulated that in the selection of the Congress candidates Mr Sanjay Gandhi's henchmen, especially from the Youth Congress, would be given preference, so that at least two hundred of the MPs could be his men. That would ensure his ascent to power.

Be it as it may, the announcement of the election electrified the atmosphere. For the first time since independence the dormant multitude, poor, illiterate, neglected and reviled, began to make its presence felt in the political arena. As leaders were released from prison to enable them to participate in the elections, the people rallied round these leaders. It was unbelievable but true. Where people before had gathered in hundreds, they gathered in tens of thousands, where they had gathered in thousands, they now gathered in hundreds of thousand. Formerly they used to be bored by public speeches. Now they would listen with rapt attention, sit through long hours of the meetings and even when the meetings were over hopefully wait for more speeches to follow till the leaders began to depart. They seemed to be eager to catch on their political education so deplorably neglected in the past. The little collection boxes, the spread towels, the drums for collection at the meetings all would be filled with small coins and currency notes, and would also receive a few earrings, watches and even lottery tickets, all tokens of implicit trust. This mood of the people, their unreserved faith, was bringing about a transformation in the stature of the leaders. The petty, scheming, feeble and lustreless leaders of the opposition suddenly shone up in the aura of mass support. They were anointed, made elect.

The instinct of self-preservation is the strongest instinct. The announcement of election instilled a new hope of survival in the political parties of the opposition. But it appeared that a united action was essential for survival. However, a move for unity, in fact a merger of the four parties, the BLD, the Jana Sangh, the Cong (O) and the Socialists, had been dragging on since before the declaration of the Emergency. But now with survival at stake the efforts at unity bore fruit with surprising speed. The unity was not confined to an electoral adjustment or united front but led to a downright merger.

That such a merger could take place at all pointed to the artificiality of the political division of the parties and the essential unity of the leaders arising from their common social background. They were hustled so suddenly into the merger only partially owing to the electoral imperative or the need to fight the dictatorship. In fact, the unity move had been there in one form or another since 1971. Ideologies were becoming a painful encumbrance in the way of personal promotion of leaders who were not too tightly tethered to class loyalties. The Emergency gave them an excuse silently to shed that encumbrance.

That it was possible to win elections without a merger became evident from the results in West Bengal or Punjab where there was only electoral understanding with the CPM and the Akalis respectively. In fact, even in 1967 when a very inadequate electoral adjustment among opposition parties had been achieved the Congress was defeated in several States (in fact, the same States in which the Congress lost this time).

To fight a dictatorship too the merger of political parties was not an essential condition. Dictatorships represent certain basic political and social attitudes, and they could be fought adequately only by clearly counterposing to them a democratic policy on these issues. Mergers only obfuscate issues unless they arise in identity of ideas. That is why in countries like France, Italy, and Spain where long and determined fight against fascism was carried on, the parties fighting fascism did not contemplate mergers but forged unity of action. The kind of merger achieved in the formation of the Janata Party could be possible only through the abandonment of their principles by some or all constituents of the party. How else could one explain the sudden convergence into one policy framework of such diametrically opposites as Socialists of radical persuasion and the Swatantrites; uncompromising secularists and the votaries of Hindu *Rashtra*? How could their convictions have melted away even without a formal debate in their respective parties ? How is it possible to fight a dictatorship in an enduring way without an adequate ideological tool ? After all, Mrs. Gandhi herself during her dictatorship was adopting some of the postures of the Jana Sangh, such as the glorification of the nation or the nuclear bomb to mystify the people. After the Bangla Desh war the RSS and the Jana Sangh were glorifying Mrs. Gandhi as *Devi Durga* and it was the very same trait that was emerging in a prominent way during the Emergency. Not surprisingly, a renowned court artist depicted her in that role in a series of paintings depicting the June events. Did the RSS and Jana Sangh suddenly mellow down? Or, did they want merely to buy time to come out in their original colours ? To the votaries of unitary India and *Akhand Bharat*, did the new slogan of decentralisation become an article of faith or merely a cloak under which a ruthless centralising would be pursued ?

With all its contradictions, or the resolution of the non-existent contradictions, a new party—the Janata Party—was formally launched and god-fathered by Mr Jayaprakash Narayan. It was formed with the merger of the BKD, the Jana Sangh, the Cong (O), and the Socialist Party. Some former leaders of the Congress, including leaders of the group known as Young Turks, also joined the party. Efforts were also afoot to have a united front and adjustment of seats with the CPM, the Akalis and the DMK. The public response to the new party and the alliance was tremendous. It was becoming clear that the popular support was overwhelming for the Janata and its allies. At this moment Mr Jagjivan Ram, who since the days of the Allahbad High Court Judgment had raised much hope and had offered only despair to the opposition, staged his grand coup.[1] He along with Mrs Nandini Satpathy, Mr K.R. Ganesh, and Mr Hemavati Nandan Behuguna announced his resignation from the Congress and decision to join hands with the Janata Party. They launched a new party, the Congress for Democracy. Now it was becoming almost certain that the Congress would be defeated. But those who sensed it kept their fingers crossed. The fear uppermost in their mind was that Mrs Gandhi would not allow the elections. or if she did allow them she would not allow them to be fair considering the popular mood.

In the election that followed the main issue as was expected became dictatorship versus democracy. Carried by the popular support and also under the impact of the terror of the Emergency, even a party like the Janata Party, which was dominated by conservative leaders, many having pronounced authoritarian streak in their personality, in its manifesto made promises which, if fulfilled, could make a good beginning for a democratic order. Among its notable promises on democratic rights were :

(3) Repeal MISA, release all political detenus, and review all unjust laws;

(7) Move to amend Article 356 to ensure that the power to impose President's Rule in a State is not misused to benefit the ruling party or any favoured faction within it;

(8) Introduce electoral reforms after a careful consideration of suggestions made by various committees, and in particular consider proposals for recall of errant legislators and for reducing election costs; as well as voting age from 21 to 18;

(13) Assure the right to peaceful and non-violent protest;

(16) Ensure that All India Radio, Doordarshan, and the Film Division are converted into genuinely autonomous bodies that are politically objective and free from governmental interference;

[1]See Appendix D.

(17) Ensure that news agencies are completely independent of the government and are not given the right to monopoly.

The elections, unexpectedly, were quite free. The public mood was so hostile to the Congress that even if the officials had wanted to rig the elections they could not have succeeded. This hostility had even affected the lower ranks of the government employees, and so no attempt to influence the outcome of the elections could have proved effective. In fact, at many places the lower ranks of the administration showed open sympathy to the candidates of the opposition parties.

The results of the elections, which were held in the third week of March, went beyond even the most optimistic expectations of the supporters of the Janata Party. In the Hindi-speaking areas the Congress was almost wiped out. In Haryana, Delhi, Uttar Pradesh, Himachal Pradesh and Bihar the Congress or its ally, the CPI, could not get even a single seat. In Madhya Pradesh and Rajasthan the Congress could secure just one in each. Similar was its fate in Punjab where the Congress or its allies failed to win a single seat. In West Bengal it could win only 3 out of 42 seats. In Orissa it got 4 out of a total of 21 seats. Even in Maharashtra, which was considered a Congress stronghold, it secured only 20 seats out of a total of 48. In areas where the impact of the Emergency or rather of the family planning drive was only lightly felt the Congress fared better. These were Karnataka and Andhra. In Kerala and Tamil Nadu, where its own strength was not much, it fared well along with its allies, the CPI and the ADMK. However, even in Andhra there was a marked decline in its support. From 71 per cent in 1971 its votes dropped to over 57 per cent in 1977. In the new Lok Sabha the Congress returned with just 153 seats against its previous tally of 352. Both Mrs Gandhi and Mr Sanjay Gandhi were defeated. The Janata-CFD total came to 300. Besides, the Janata had the support of the 22 members of the CPM and 9 members of the Akali Dal. This brought to an end the nineteen-month-old dictatorship and the thirty-year rule of the Congress at the Centre. A Janata government in coalition with the Akalis was formed with Mr Morarji Desai,

who himself had spent 19 months in Mrs. Gandhi's prison,
becoming the Prime Minister.

The day of the formation of the new ministry was marked
by jubilation all over the country. People heaved a sigh of
relief. Their only concern now was to see that the days of the
Emergency did not return. Their determination to keep the
Congress out of power was once again demonstrated in the
June election to the nine State Assemblies which had been
dissolved some time back. Again the Congress received a
heavy battering. This time Janata got the majority in Bihar,
Orissa, Madhya Pradesh, Rajasthan, Haryana, Delhi, Himachal
Pradesh and Uttar Pradesh. Its former allies, the CPM-led
United Front and the Akalis, had the majority in West Bengal
and Punjab respectively. Thus people ensured that for the
coming five years not only at the Centre but also in these
States the Congress was prevented from coming to power. But
more important, it also forestalled any move to get a Congress
nominee elected to the highest office of the state, the Presidency.

Chapter Seven

The Challenge

Nonetheless, he knew that the tale he had to tell could not be one of final victory. It could be only the record of what had had to be done, and what assuredly would have to be done again in the the never-ending fight against terror and its relentless onslaughts, despite their personal afflictions, by all who while unable to be saints, but refusing to bow down to pestilences, strive their utmost to be healers.

Albert Camus, *The Plague*

The poor illiterate and semi-literate masses have for the first time made their voice felt on the issue of political liberty. And the credit mainly goes to them to have liberated a demoralised and disoriented elite that had abandoned the very ground which fostered its chief claim to the leadership of the nation. This time it was clear that people had not voted on economic issues, though these might have had peripheral appeal for some. If anything, on purely economic grounds the slogans of the Congress and its ally, the CPI, were more alluring. And though the claims of the gains of the Emergency had been exaggerated beyond measure, the drop in prices of essential commodities, which coincided with the imposition of the Emergency did provide some relief to the poor people. Notwithstanding all this the people voted for freedom. That certainly does much credit to their judgment and belies that contemptuous theory that poor people need only bread, and free institutions are not for them.

But the fact that the people identified themselves with the government led by the Janata Party and its allies, has also roused expectations from it. They might not have expected economic gains at the time they voted. Since these parties are now in power they cannot but look to them for the basic needs of life. If frustrated, they may use the newly-won freedom to press forward with their demands. That again will be the test for the substance of the newly-acquired democratic power. If they find these efforts fruitless, they may again slip back into apathy and spell the doom of democracy. How the new administration reacts to them will greatly determine the future of democracy in the country.

Only a few months back people took democracy as all but lost in this country. It was saved because the common people became aware of the value of freedom following the excesses of the Emergency especially in regard to the family planning drive. But had there been no elections possibly the country would have gone through a rash of sporadic protests and uprisings followed by brutal suppression, as happened in Pakistan. But a serious miscalculation by Mrs Gandhi led to the elections which proved her undoing. Often such events and decisions radically alter the course of history. But we cannot always count on such misdirection of policy, as the forced sterilisation drive, or such miscalculation as was made by Mrs Gandhi about the elections, to win back lost freedom. So it would be prudent not to take chances with our freedom a second time. That means we have to build a stable base of freedom.

Though the events following 26 June 1975 had come as a bolt from the blue, many of the features of that event were neither sudden nor entirely new. What were those features? (1) The preventive detention of a large number of leaders; (2) arrest on trumped-up charges of a much larger number of political activists; (3) imposition of ban on public meetings and processions; (4) arbitrary use of magistracy and police to suppress all political activities of the opposition parties; (5) denial of the right to move the courts when arrested under MISA 16(A); and (6) strict censorship of the Press.

As we have noted in an earlier chapter, the preventive detention on a large scale was already quite in vogue. People in
their thousands had been arrested under the Preventive Detention Act or the Defence of India Rules, both under Mr Nehru
and Mr Lal Bahadur Shastri, and of course under Mrs Indira
Gandhi even before she became a dictator. It was the same
story about the arrest of political leaders on trumped-up
charges, when it suited the administration. This used to be the
most common form of pre-emptive action by the administration
whenever some mass agitation was apprehended. Many of the
men in the new Janata set-up, including the Prime Minister
Mr Morarji Desai, were among the architects of this administrative device. What appeared especially shocking and
unethical this time was that the blow had also fallen for the
first time on men who had known so far only to hand out such
dispensation to others. Besides, this time the police dragnet was
spread wider to include hitherto untouched categories of men.

In the case of the MISA detenus there certainly was a difference this time. They could not move a court if detained
under MISA 16(A). But in preventive detention the chances of
release in any case depended only on technical flaws and at no
time could preventive detention have been challenged on the
basis of the substance of the charges. The courts in the past
have been known in the cases of detention both to release the
detenus and also to confirm the detention.

Imposition of ban on public meetings, procession and even
imposition of curfew was not a new feature peculiar to the
Emergency rule under Mrs Gandhi. These had been quite in
vogue since independence and were often used purely for the
convenience of the administration. Even their use to promote
the interests of the ruling party was not unusual. Similarly, the
partisan attitude of the administration in dealing with political parties had long been incorporated in our political life.
The leaders of the Congress Party almost since the advent of
freedom had acquired a prescriptive right to tutor the civil
servants and police officers at various levels in the performance
of their duty. Extra-constitutional authority was not wholly
a new creation of Mr Sanjay Gandhi, though he stretched it
to heights where it stood out most conspicuously.

The most unnerving thing was the total blackout of political news through the censorship. In its magnitude and effect it was wholly new. Nothing of the kind had been attempted at any time before, even during British rule. As people groped in the dark, fearful phantoms of all kinds assailed them. Lack of information and the resulting insecurity made terror an inner force deriving nourishment from men's own imagination. The suffering under such a situation gained in poignancy as the feeling of total forlornness enveloped a man. He felt he had not only to suffer or die, but suffer unnoticed without any hope of succour, as his cry would not go beyond himself. This certainly brings into bold relief the role of free Press in a democratic order. Many authoritarian features were already there in our system, but they made themselves felt in their full force only when the freedom of the Press was totally snuffed out.

But did this freedom go all at once? We who remained near the centre of things and formed part of the dominant section of the nation are prone to think so. We never suffered any serious handicap at the hands of the Press, because it always spoke for what was supposed to be the interest of the dominant section and so by implication for the whole people. But all along there were areas on our periphery, even small crevices, right in the midst of the nation's heartland which have suffered black-outs when they were most in need of spotlight. In fact, the distant lights had begun to go out long before the final darkness descended on 26 June 1975.

Under some misapprehension of partiotism or some community of interests our newsmen have tried generally to move in tandem with the powers that be. And that loyalty has made their loyalty to truth less than total when reporting events which are likely to embarrass those in authority. How many of our newsmen have done, for example, any investigative reporting about the real conditions of life in Nagaland? The official stories dished out, which is the staple dessert of most news reporting about that place, tell us practically nothing. Did our Press seek to find the truth about Kashmir, about the feelings and grievances of the people there? We may lull ourselves into false complacency through reassuring reports. But

can we assuage the feelings of the people there unless we have
gone fully into the depths of their feelings? But we have only
known the official trash aired through the Press. How much
remained under the fig-leaf in Bangla Desh operation or in
Sikkim, when it became a part of India we will perhaps never
know because the sense of duty to the nation of our newsmen
would never allow them to disclose the truth. Truth may often
be dangerous, of course. Mr B.G. Verghese of *The Hindustan
Times* had to lose his job for just one critical editorial on Sikkim.
How many newsmen had the courage to investigate the atrocities committed in the name of fighting the Naxalite insurgency?
Though this kind of operation went on for over the best part
of a decade, in which every kind of cruelty was perpetrated on
helpless people, only a few stray reports appeared of these
happenings. For the rest we were regaled with the stories of
the atrocities of the Naxalites and the horrors committed by
the peasants against the landlords. Only now when the Tarkunde Commission, which had the blessing of the new administration in Delhi, has blown the gaff that the Press seems to
have become alive to that kind of dastardly action of the police.

The upshot of this kind of partial news coverage has been
that the people who are victims of such black-outs, misrepre-
sentations or cover-ups have lived or perhaps are still living
under the kind of terror we have only temporarily experienced.
We might have ignored the tragedy of these second or third
rate citizens of our great country, but we have to be concerned
about their fate because ultimately that affects our fate too.
The men who indulge in this kind of misreporting gradually
become insensible to human suffering in all forms. Under
strong inducement, be it from fear, patronage or venality, such
men will misrepresent or lie about even those whom they now
think they serve. The fact that almost the entire journalistic
outfit continued its uninterrupted career from the pre-Emergency
days, through the Emergency, to the present, is not without its
significance. Perhaps all the three kinds of inducement were at
work. Fear perhaps was the dominant one; but the other two
were not always absent.

There has been much talk of dismantling the whole apparatus of dictatorship. The question that immediately comes to

one's mind is: Which apparatus? Mrs Gandhi hardly created any
new apparatus. She used the same apparatus which she found
ready to her hand, and it is the same apparatus which is serving
the new incumbents in office. There has been far more con-
tinuity in the mode of government between the one that preceded Mrs Gandhi and the one that was in operation during
the Emergency than the present rulers are inclined to admit.
The seed of dictatorship was always there in that old apparatus.
That seed has not been uprooted even now and only lies waiting
to germinate and throw up its noxious foliage whenever conditions permit it.

One powerful factor ceaselessly pushing us towards authoritarianism is the extremely narrow base of the political elite in
a country where it has to rule with the consent of the vast
multitude of poor and deprived masses. The elite's way of life
and its ambition link it closely to the economic vested interests which do their utmost to prevent such measures as would
improve the condition of the common man. The political elite
has only two choices to be able to keep itself in power. Either
it has to wring itself free from the vested interests and move
to bring about rapid improvement in the conditions of the poor
in order to widen its base of support, or carry on a holding
operation with mystifying appeals of national glory, traditions,
military parades, and pageantry. The first is an extremely
difficult course, but the only one for an enduring democratic
order. The temptation of luxury is too great. But in the condition of India it could be brought only at the cost of freedom.
The choice of freedom means a clean break with the tradition
of a century in the style of life of the elite. The other path is
one of inevitable decline of the role of the elite and the democratic polity if the latter is identified with the former. People
cannot always be fobbed off with high-sounding slogans or
promises. Sooner or later, their pressure will mount and there
will be counter pressure from the authoritarian forces within
the state institutions and there will be a tendency to revert to
the rule of the prison and the bullet. This will lead either to
the kind of dictatorship we just had or to a more fundamental
though barbarous change arising in the frustration of the masses, the kind of change witnessed in Cambodia where the

entire city-bred, luxury-loving populace was driven out of cities and scattered around to fend for itself as best as it could or perish.

The quarter century of the development of the country, as we have earlier noted, was in the direction of a rule of intimidation. Mrs Gandhi did no more than give the final blow to a system which was tending more and more to a hollow formality.

The play of personalities masks the pattern behind the usually confused denouement of events. Apparently Mrs Gandhi was the sole villain in the drama that unfolded into the Emergency. In a certain sense she indeed was. But what role may be attributed to the elite as a whole and the various wings of the administration which defied all law and propriety to promote her to an unchallenged power? It would be difficult to find who was the principal and who the agent in this chain of cause and consequence. Looking at the entire context it was the upper class-elite combination which wanted to use Mrs Gandhi as the most appropriate agent to subserve their interests. She perfectly fitted the matrix with her love of luxury, trappings of Westernisation, lack of vision or clear political convictions. Her great merits were only a later discovery. What had she done in the first place to be elevated to prime ministership? Apparently, it was her weakness which commended her for the job. But having attained a degree of control over the apparatus, she also used that complex to promote herself to a dictatorial authority. Mrs Gandhi's re-emergence into politics certainly constitutes now a danger as she may again become a rallying point for all authoritarian trends. But her retirement from politics does not end the danger of dictatorship, because faced with popular threat to its privileges the upper class-elitist complex may find other agents to take over her mantle.

The preservation of democracy in India, looking at the odds against it, is a challenging task. It is a challenge in the main to the people who claim to be the nation's intellectual and moral preceptors. But it is a challenge also to the political leaders, who have all along spoken in the name of democracy and now hold power. For them it is an opportunity to prove their loyalty to this ideal. It is, to be sure, not convenient. But to rule democratically has not been convenient even in the best of circumstances. The deprivations and the dangers that adherence to democratic values engenders have to be faced if the system is to survive.

When we look at the few months during which the Janata Party has been in power, the picture is not very encouraging. Of course it is too short a period to judge a government. But it is a long enough period to judge the trends or the moral tone of the authority. Austerity was made a key-word in its election campaign. But it is difficult to find it anywhere in a remarkable way. Looking around one hardly feels that the nation has just emerged from a deeply-shaking experience. The masses who for a while had felt drawn near the centre of political events are again being relegated to their old places. The men who till the Lok Sabha poll had fawned on Mrs Gandhi and worked for the Congress are being invited to the Janata Party and are already forming a part of the new court. The economic policies that have emerged so far remain the same uninspiring exercise in generalities.

However disheartening the trends of economic thinking may be, it may still be argued that only time could prove whether economic policies have been in the right direction. But the same cannot be said about some of the policies of the government in political matters.

The dissolution of the nine Assemblies through a Presidential order was a severe blow to the autonomy of the States. The cloak of morality in which Mr Charan Singh sought to cover himself looked indecently transparent after the executive fiat. Substantially it might be true that the governments in these States had lost the support of the people as reflected in the Lok Sabha elections. But in principle to say that a State government automatically loses public support if the elections of a different body go against the party in power in the State, cuts at the root of State autonomy. Though in the last election the issues had been narrowed to one—democracy versus dictatorship—it is not always that the Assembly and Lok Sabha elections are fought on the same issue. Mr Jayaprakash Narayan's call to elect the same party to the State Assemblies as at the Centre was all the more deplorable as he commands great respect in the public eye. If that principle were accepted, no party other than the one ruling at the Centre would survive. This would be the end of the federal system. With the present precedent the future of the State governments depends entirely on the whims of the Centre. This time the State governments were dismissed even without observing the formality of going through the reports of the Governors, a normal practice followed in the past. Even the earlier practice gave rise to a great deal of arbitrariness as the Governors were themselves the nominees of the Centre and often willing to oblige. But going by the latest example the central government has just to convince itself, without any definite channel of information about the state of things in a State to impose its rule.

For the future of democracy the autonomy of the States is fo paramount importance. So long as the States are fully autonomous the hands of an authoritarian government at the Centre could be effectively held off where the rights and liberties of the citizens are concerned. Even during the last Emergency the governments of Gujarat and Tamil Nadu, even under the existing limitations on the autonomous powers of the State, were able to prevent many of the excesses of the Emergency as long as the non-Congress governments were allowed to remain in power. Mr Charan Singh's action in dissolving the State Assembles, whatever its immediate benefits, was a big blow to the future of democracy in the country. It is through such short-cuts and expediencies that a democratic system goes to perdition.

Similarly, on the question of release of political prisoners and repeal of MISA the Janata government continues to drag its feet, even though about the latter it has made a clear commitment in its election manifesto. What is worse, barely three months after assuming power it used MISA to arrest its political opponents. Prior to the Assembly elections in Kashmir, where Janata's chances were not too bright, a large number of arrests were made, 132 of them according to an official report under MISA in the week ending 23 June 1977. According to the National Conference sources over 2000 of their workers had been arrested. The resulting terror is conceivable. The following report by S. Viswan published in *The Statesman* of 1 July 1977 gives some idea of the reign of terror:

The large-scale preventive arrests have in the past four or five days produced the new fear psychosis. All the three major parties—the National Conference, the Congress and the Janata Party—have charged the police with making unwarranted and indiscriminate arrests of their workers. The number of workers of each party detained during the past few days varies, but it would seem that the National Conference has contributed the most man power to the prisons. According to reports, the pre-poll arrests have caused not only resentment in the ranks of various parties, but have made political workers so nervous at the thought of being picked up that many do not sleep in their own homes at night, but keep moving from place to place...

We may realise the enormity of it all by a comparison. If Mrs Gandhi had conducted her election on the same scale she would have put sixty to seventy thousand Janata workers in prison on the eve of the Lok Sabha elections and set the others scurrying to evade arrest. Janata might still have won. But one cannot be too sure.

These developments coming so soon after the defeat of a dictator for just such crimes should be disturbing.

There is also another disquieting sign. The old sycophancy has gone, but a new one is developing. People are fast switching sides and are being welcomed with open arms by the new rulers. Like all hangers-on they are propitiating and pleasing and consequently misleading. The newspapers are assuming a new kind of self-censorship though their preferences have reversed. But that only strengthens the power of the rulers over the ruled. The identification of the Press with state power, whether voluntary or involuntary, is equally damaging to the interests of the people. Press can play its proper role when it acts as people's watch-dog, i.e., a critical role towards authority.

The foregoing discussion would show that none of the basic problems that beset our democratic system has been solved or is being tackled with the urgency it deserves. It appears that no apparatus of dictatorship is in the process of getting dismantled. Even the authoritarian outlook is not being discarded. The new rulers are equipped with all the instruments of absolute power and they have not so far shown excessive caution in their use on the few occasions when such caution was warranted. So there is little reason for euphoria.

All that can be said is that people have won a respite. But whether this becomes long or lasting will depend on the efforts that are made ceaselessly to erase from the system the elements of arbitrary power. It is not going to be an easy task. The new rulers seem to be stepping into the shoes of the old ones. The people have to be warned against the new trend. If necessary, they will have to fight to protect the newly-won rights from every kind of onslaught against them. That is a challenge the people must face if the country is to be saved from slipping back into dictatorship once again.

APPENDIX A

Text of the letter written by Mr George Fernandes from prison to Mr N.G. Goray on 14 December 1976 on the proposed opposition talks with Mrs Indira Gandhi.

My dear Nanasaheb,

The newspapers report that you are attending a meeting of opposition parties called by Mr Karunanidhi to initiate talks with Mrs Gandhi. According to my information, some talks are on at the moment between Mrs Gandhi's nominees and some important leaders of some opposition parties. I also learn that some kind of proposals amounting to a sell-out have also been submitted by these opposition leaders. I am sure you will make it clear to these opposition leaders' meeting that as far as the Socialist Party is concerned, it is committed to continue the struggle against Mrs Gandhi's dictatorship to its logical end and can never compromise on certain fundamental issues, like withdrawal of the Emergency and scrapping of MISA, release of all political prisoners and others held without trial, freedom of the Press, independence of the judiciary, immediate dissolution of the illegitimate Lok Sabha and holding of elections after fulfilling certain preconditions to ensure a free poll, repeal of all constitutional amendments adopted since 26 June 1975. The recent special convention of the party held in Bombay has, if anything, endorsed the line of struggle always pursued by the party. I also hope you will be able to persuade the opposition leaders to get their parties to direct their members in the Lok Sabha to resign their seats forthwith and join forces to wage a relentless struggle to overthrow the dictatorship. A copy of my letter to JP is enclosed herewith.

   With greetings,

           Yours sincerely,
           George Fernandes.

Mr N.G. Goray.

Copy to : Surendra Mohan, General Secretary, Socialist Party.

**Text of the letter written by Mr George Fernandes to
Mr Jayaprakash Narayan on 14 December 1976.**

My dear Jayaprakashji,

  There are certain aspects of the present situation that have disturbed me and alarmed me. First, there is the orchestration of statements by many sundry leaders and some leader writers urging you to call off the movement. Second, one sees constant efforts by some busy-bodies to somehow or the other secure an invitation to sit across the table with Mrs Gandhi. Third, there is a stubborn refusal to realise that Vinoba's first loyalty is to the Court and that he will never lift a little finger to help the fighters for freedom and democracy in the country. Fourth, there is reluctance to make an honest evaluation of the changes that have taken place in our body-politic since Mrs Gandhi turned dictator on 26 June 1975. Concomitant with all this is the delusion that Mrs Gandhi is still not a dictator. A recent refrain from those who seek to have a dialogue is that the first task before JP and others is to secure the release of those in prisons.

  I had hoped that this growing cacophony of normalisers is but only a manifestation of the frustration and despondency of some of the leaders and not one of those diabolical moves of the dictator to drive a wedge in the ranks of those opposed to her dictatorship, sow confusion among the masses and demoralise those who are uncompromising in their fight. This move to negotiate has, I believe, been motivated by a desire to prevent or in any case postpone the creation of one party through a merger of various parties of the opposition by presenting a new set of priorities.

The frantic efforts that are being made, and a series of meet-ings that have been arranged of opposition party leaders have confirmed my fears of a 'sell-out'. I could not believe that any responsible leaders from any party could formally put down the kind of terms that are reported to have been suggested as the basis for talks that are scheduled for the next few days. Neither the demand to revoke the Emergency nor for the release of all political prisoners surprisingly is set for negotiations. Whatever the result of these talks, it would affect the already low morale and sagging determination of political workers and others who have been opposing the dictatorship.

I must say the opposition parties in India have neither learnt nor unlearnt anything since 26 June 1975. When will they realise that they are facing a woman who will never surrender power? Can they not see that if Nehru went about grooming his daughter in a subtle and sophisticated way to succeed him, the mother lacks even a modicum of shame while indulging in a crude and vulgar exercise to annoint her son as the successor? This is not to say that Nehru's method was commendable or was less dishonourable, but only to point out that like then so now the opposition refuses to understand the designs of the ruling clique. Over the years, opposition politics in India has been of reacting to the initiatives of the ruling party and of never taking the initiative on its own and making the ruling coterie run for its chairs. In the mid-sixties, Dr Lohia took the initiative, united the opposition by dragging them literally by the scruff of their necks and routed the Congress in 1967. But since then, except for the initiative which the youth took in Gujarat and later in Bihar, there has hardly been an effort to confront the Congress by the opposition parties. The develop-ments since 26 June 1975 indicate that the opposition leaders lack not only in perspective but also in nerve. Or else how can anyone say that the primary task today is to secure the release of those in prisons? This is not the stuff that can oppose and overthrow a dictatorship, if anything, this is the stuff that breeds and nourishes dictators.

I am aware of your own frustrations with the opposition leaders, and also of the kind of the pressures they are building on you. But I want you to know that there are people who are committed to carry the fight against the dictatorship to the bitter end and for as long as is necessary. I believe that there can be no compromise with the dictatorship. I believe that there are certain issues which are simply non-negotiable. These are: revocation of the Emergency and scrapping of MISA; release of all political prisoners and others held without trial; freedom of the Press; independence of the Judiciary; immediate dissolution of the illegitimate Lok Sabha and the holding of elections after fulfilling certain pre-conditions to ensure a fair poll; and repeal of all constitutional amendments adopted since 26 June 1975.

I know that Mrs Gandhi will accept none of these terms. If she can accept these conditions now, she need not have, in the first place, usurped power and become a dictator. And it is not merely that it is impossible for her to reverse what she has done. With an opposition that does not show much will to fight, what is there for her to be worried about? So what precisely do the 'negotiators' want to 'negotiate' about, even if they realise at this last moment to add to their demands for discussion at the negotiating table?

Instead of spending their time drafting statements seeking negotiations with Mrs Gandhi and being overenthusiastic at the prospect of talks on whatever terms, I wish the opposition parties applied their collective mind to build an effective movement among all sections of our people to resist the dictatorship. The time appears to be favourable for such efforts to be successful.

For all her bombast, Mrs Gandhi is today more isolated from the people than she ever was. Her credibility is at its nadir. I am told that recently in Delhi even doctors rushed to the schools and took their children away believing that Mrs Gandhi is sterilising them. She and her propagandists say that prices are falling, while in Delhi in the four weeks beginning from the first week of November to the first week of December there has been an increase of ten to twenty per cent in the prices of consumer goods. Even in Delhi's Super Bazar, the dictator's much touted fair price shop of the Capital, mustard oil was selling at Rs. 12.15 a Kg on 1 December, compared to Rs. 10.20 on 1 November. In this one month vanaspati has gone up from

Rs. 8.15 to Rs. 8.50 a Kg, packed vanaspati from 9.90 to 10.15 a Kg, pure ghee from Rs. 25.50 to Rs. 26.25 a Kg. Two hundred grams of coconut oil cost Rs. 4.65 on 1 December compared to Rs. 4.25 in the last week of November. The same with the prices of dals. In the above period of one month, a Kg of Moong (whole) is up from Rs. 2.15 to Rs. 2.30, Urad (whole) from Rs. 2.65 to Rs. 2.80, Masur (Red) from Rs. 2.45 to Rs. 2.80, Rajma Chitra from Rs. 2.60 to Rs. 2.95. *The Economic Times* index of wholesale prices of commodities (base 1969-70: 100) which was 158.5 on 9 December 1975 stood at 179.2 on 9 December 1976.

Her Radio has become a permanent joke. The censored Press and the Samacharred news do not fool the people any more. The all-pervading fear that she succeeded in instilling among the people is still there; but in Bombay, Poona, Bangalore, West Bengal and Tamil Nadu, there has been a series of strike actions by industrial workers. The number of police firings in Uttar Pradesh alone during the last few months of the sterilisation drive are said to be more than one hundred with over a thousand fatal casualities. Last month, in a speech in the Lok Sabha, Shibbanlal Saxena said that in his constituency of Gorakhpur police had opened fire on people in several places to force them into sterilisation camps. Of course, the speech was censored. In West Bengal and Orissa, her sycophants are fighting like hungry dogs over a bone. In Maharashtra and Karnataka, her party is a house divided. In Gujarat, her party legislators came to blows on who should be the Chief Minister. Her ministers in Orissa and West Bengal are issuing Press statements accusing each other of being "anti-social elements" who indulge in "anti-social activities." This is the house Mrs Gandhi lives in. Granted that the bureaucracy and the repressive organs of state power are continuing to prop her petticoat dictatorship, but are there not enough signs to indicate that like all dictatorships everywhere her dictatorship too finally will be consigned to the garbage heap?

I am sorry if I have rambled a bit. But I think it is necessary to record my total disenchantment with some of our friends. It is my conviction that the future of our country will be shaped by those who are willing to stake their everything to restore democracy and the rule of law. The compromisers and others who are seeking the soft options will succeed only in giving some legitimacy and hence credibility and respectability to Mrs Gandhi's dictatorship.

In this context, I am at a loss to understand the mind of those who continue to maintain their membership of the Lok Sabha even while they criticise for record that it is a House which has lost its mandate. Why should any one take cognisance of their criticism when they have no qualms in deriving whatever petty privileges they can as members of that illegitimate Lok Sabha? This split mind of the opposition is Mrs Gandhi's strength.

I am glad that the Socialist Party's special convention that met in Bombay at the end of November has resolved to give all support to your efforts to unite the four parties of the opposition. If such unity is not forthcoming, the party has said that it will go along with you in the formation of a new party. In the present frame of mind of the leaders of parties which were to merge and their anxiety to reach a settlement at the cost of giving up our fundamental demands, I believe that it is not desirable to make further attempts to bring about a merger. One of the basic points of agreements for the merger was the struggle for the restoration of the *status quo ante* 26 June 1975, and it is clear that no party other than the Socialist Party is willing now to adhere to this basic objective, and the Socialist Party cannot agree to a merger unless there is agreement over this fundamental question. The political resolution adopted by the Bombay convention of the party has directed the party members to address themselves to the task of "training and organisation of the cadres and the widest possible mass contact for a long and sustained struggle for the restoration of democracy."

Since June 1974, I have been urging you to launch a political party, and I have committed myself, despite some reservations and a little hostility from many of my party comrades, to work for the success of that effort. At the meeting of opposition parties convened by you in November 1974 in Delhi, I had circulated a long note (which was later issued in pamphlet form) i nwhich I had publicly appealed to you to launch a new party. I am aware of the handicaps you face because of the state of your health, but I believe that you owe it to posterity to bring under one banner all those who are pledged to fight against the dictatorship and are committed to the creation of a democratic and egalitarian society in India.

I am deliberately refraining from making any suggestions about the forms and future course of struggle. I have said enough on this during my days in the underground and done what I believed was needed and was within my capacity. I have no regrets and I can never have any reasons to revise my views. I am sure that our youth, workers and intellectuals will keep forging new and adequate instruments of struggle and succeed in overthrowing the dictatorship. There have been signs in recent weeks of restlessness and defiance in many circles, signs which should gladden your heart as they have put more hope in mine.

In the context of the negotiations that are under way and the general anxiety for a settlement that is apparent from the attitude of the leadership of most opposition parties, it is necessary to make it clear that the Socialist Party cannot agree to participate in such negotiations, nor will it agree to join other parties in the move to withdraw the struggle against the dictatorship. The Socialist Party has made its position clear in the past and has endorsed it at the recent Bombay convention. As the Chairman of the Socialist Party, I will not be a party to the repudiation of what has been an article of faith and which has received unqualified and unanimous support and endorsement from the rank and file. I think it my duty to make the position of the Socialist Party and of my own clear to you as I understand that you are being pressurised to agree to the withdrawal of the struggle by the Lok Sangharsh Samiti.

Please take care of your health. I do not have to tell you how much all of us think of you and pray for your health. With kindest regards,

Yours sincerely,
Sd/-
George Fernandes.

Mr Jayaprakash Narayan,
Patna.

PS: A few questions which are bothering me: Why have the
negotiators become so vocal when Mrs Gandhi is having serious
problems in Orissa and West Bengal where the CPI-supported
Chief Ministers and their coteries are under attack by their own
partymen, and when from Delhi to Chinchpokli, Congressmen
are vying with each other in issuing statements telling their CPI
tail to stop wagging the Congress dog? Is Mrs Gandhi trying
to tell something to the Russians through proxy by encouraging
the negotiators whom she branded till a few days ago as
"fascists"? Or is she trying to tell the American and Western
capitalists that India is theirs to plunder and when it comes to
ideology, the fascists of yesterday will be her friends tom-
morrow?

APPENDIX B

**Note from Mr George Fernandes for consideration by the
National Committee of the Socialist Party**

It is one month since the opposition parties made their collective
overtures to Mrs Gandhi requesting her to invite them to the
negotiating table. Biju Patnaik and some others even spelt out
the terms of surrender in their "approach papers" and other
communications to the dictator's representatives. Characteristi-
cally, the dictator has kept the opposition's "negotiators"
guessing, while she and her more important minions like Bansilal
and Om Mehta continue to fire their broadsides against the
opposition. In the meanwhile, the dictator also continues with
her litany of lies about their being no Press censorship and that
except a "handful" of opposition leaders all those in detention
have been released.

In the last one week there have been some significant releases
of opposition workers in several States. There are indications
that there may be some more releases in the coming few days.
At the same time, there is speculation that Mrs Gandhi may
call a general election in March 1977.

Those who have been wanting to make up with the dictator
will see in these releases and in the rumours of an impending
election "the restoration of normalcy". They will now plead
with fervour for the immediate merger of opposition parties and
would want to quickly get on with the job of distribution of
seats for the elections.

Having tantalised the opposition with hopes of talks to restore normalcy and having made Biju Patnaik and his party submit a surrender document called the "approach paper" and in the process, created rifts and misunderstandings not only in the ranks of the opposition parties, but also among people in general. Mrs Gandhi now seems confident enough about the success of her grand strategy to acquire a legitimacy that she has been in search of since she became a dictator on 26 June 1975.

Let us face it. There is neigher a legal compulsion nor any political necessity for her to have the elections today. What she needs is the firming up and brightening of the constitutional and democratic facade which she sadly lacks today. If the elections give her an overwhelming majority and such opposition as there may be is weak and has an understanding with her, she will have achieved besides formal constitutional legitimacy, *moral* authority. She will prove, thereby, to opinion abroad and such as is left in India, that she is the democratically chosen leader of the country and head of government. She will also prove that the opposition, its tactics, and its charges against her have no support among the people.

Therefore, she needs the elections desperately to clothe her with legal and moral authority to excercise unrestrained power. Her need has become even more because of the internal contradictions that are developing into a threat to her authority within the government and party.

In his letter of 14 December 1976, to Nanasaheb Goray on the eve of the Delhi meeting of the opposition, Jayaprakash Narayan said:

"I believe that in case government revokes the Emergency, withdraws various restrictions imposed on the freedom of the Press through various enactments and other measures, restores other civil liberties including the right of assembly, puts political activity outside the purview of the MISA and restores the right of habeas corpus and of judicial review further circumscribed by the 42nd amendment, releases all political prisoners unconditionally in good time, and announces a firm date for holding a free general election, the opposition should have no hesitation in co-operating in the restoration of normalcy."

The meeting of opposition leaders took place in Delhi on December 15, 16 and 17. Though JP's letter was before this meeting, the opposition leaders chose to ignore JP's advice, and Asoka Mehta went on to report to his party's Working Committee that "the discussion (between opposition leaders) got some relevance when the BLD representatives reported about the initial talks they had (about a dialogue) with some representatives of the government." Asoka Mehta's letter to his Working Committee further went on to state that the meeting of opposition leaders "approved" the approach (approach note of the BLD to the government) and "welcomed a dialogue". Unfortunately, the participants at the meeting not only ignored JP's advice, but seem to have kept it a secret, while a three-sentence formal latter from JP to Karunanidhi was widely published to imply that JP welcomed the kind of negotiations and approved of the terms of settlement which was said to be imminent. Later, Surendra Mohan was to state in a letter to Biju Patnaik (on 4 January 1977) that the BLD's "approach paper" had not been approved by the opposition leaders' meeting and dissociated the Socialist Party from this "Approach Paper".

The over-anxiety of the opposition to seek a meeting with Mrs Gandhi, on any terms and the impression that was promoted that the impending negotiatings had JP's approval impelled JP to address another letter to all opposition leaders on 29 December enclosing to each of them a copy of his earlier letter (of 14 December) to Nanasaheb Goray. In this letter JP reiterated and elaborated his earlier position.

"As for the question of dialogue with the government, I have already indicated my views in my letter to Shri Goray (copy enclosed). I would, however, like to emphasise that the dialogue to be meaningful should begin only after all political prisoners have been released unconditionally, and civil liberties and Press freedoms have been fully restored so as to suspend the agitation launched in 1975 by the Sangharsh Samiti. This does not mean that we approve or accept the recent constitutional amendments rushed through the present Parliament. We reserve our right to educate and rally public opinion against such of the amendments as violate the basic structure

of the consitution and/or militate against the democratic
rights of the people. We must also demand that the government announce forthwith the date of the next General
Election and take positive steps, *in consultation with the
opposition* to ensure a free and fair poll."

It is obvious from both communications of Jayaprakash
Narayan that he too is keen on elections. But he is not for
elections at any cost and on any conditions. Elections must be
free and fair, and positive steps to ensure that they are free and
fair must be taken in consultation with the opposition. But this
must be preceded by (1) revocation of Emergency; (2) withdrawal
of various restrictions on freedom of the Press through various
enactments and other measures; (3) restoration of civil liberties
including the right of assembly; (4) putting political activity out of
the purview of the MISA and restoration of the right of habeas
corpus and of judicial review now circumscribed by the 42
amendment; and (5) release of all political prisoners in good
time.

I wonder if the opposition parties have the same clarity of
mind and firmness of approach to these questions as JP has. If
the few published statements of some leaders of the opposition
are any indication, most of them seem eager to get into the
election business as soon as possible. Even Nanasaheb Goray
reportedly told the Press a few days ago that if Mrs Gandhi
announces the poll, we are willing to take part in it. Asoka
Mehta put out a circular in November '75, even when he was
still in detention, asking the opposition to nominate its candidates and appointing a committee to collect funds. Since his
release he has been too often reported in the Press urging Mrs
Gandhi to hold elections.

I do not wish to elaborate here on the general political situation in the country. That has been done too often to require
repetition. But, nevertheless, let me reiterate a few obvious
truths. In the conditions now prevailing, the lifting of Press
censorship, and formal freedom to indulge in "constitutional and
responsible" political activity have no meaning. Lifting of the
Emergency does not restore the freedoms that have been taken
away by constitutional amendments and by the adoption of

special laws that have eroded fundamental rights. Release from jail will not mean ability to operate freely and meaningfully in the political field. Freeing the Press of censorship still leaves the Press at the mercy of the Publication of Objectionable Matters Act. Above all, the fear created extensively and deeply will be a deterrent against the exercise of even the limited freedom that may follow from legal repeals of the Emergency, Press censorship, etc. What guarantee is there that those who do not "behave" are not clamped back in jails, or such newpapers as may express objectivity, independence and courage will not be penalised?

Therefore merely lifting of Emergency, release of political prisoners, or repeal of Press censorship will not ensure free and fair elections. The minimum is the restoration of status quo ante 26 June 1975. And such restoration should be at least for nine months to a year before elections are held to enable political parties to rebuild their organisations, the political cadres to be able to function effectively, the Press to shed its fear of conse- quences, and above all for people to respond freely and without fear to the call of the opposition.

Without these conditions, the message of the opposition can- not be delivered through the Press, the platform or other means of publicity. The wherewithal to organise a campaign would be difficult to secure. After all, even before 26 June 1975, transport, printing facilities and such facilities as electricity for public meetings could be made unavailable with a frown from the ruling party or of the administration at its behest. It is doubtful whether opposition parties would be able to get the services of an adequate number of workers to man polling stations, and in some constituencies, candidates. As for monetary resources, who would dare or even wish to donate to the oppo- sition against the wishes of Mrs Gandhi. She herself will have no difficulty in getting as much as she needs, openly and legitimately, now that the ban on company donations has been lifted.

Unless conditions are restored to those prevailing on 25 June 1975 and at least nine months to a year passes with normal free conditions prevailing, participating in elections would be a disaster. It is extremely doubtful if the four principal parties

can get fifty members into Parliament if these two conditions
are not met.

A nine-point "Tentative Note for Possible Discussion with
Government" drafted by Mr Tarkunde takes care of some of
these questions. The opposition must not accept anything less
than what is laid down in that Note and as stated earlier, a
time of nine months to one year must be there from the restoration of *status quo ante* 26 June 1975 to the holding of elections.

Here I would like to make a point on what is meant by a free
and fair poll. The people's March to Parliament on 6 March
1975, led by Jayaprakash Narayan presented a charter of
demands to the Speaker of the Lok Sabha and to the Chairman
of the Rajya Sabha which, inter alia, made the following sub-
missions on electoral reforms:

Free and fair Elections: It is essential that Parliament and
Assemblies be made more responsive to popular aspirations.
Elections must not be allowed to be influenced by use of official
machinery, money power and recourse to force. We therefore,
urge that:

1. The unanimous recommendations of the Joint Parliamentary Committee on Electoral Reforms in which
   members of the ruling party were also present should be
   implemented without delay.

2. The government must not be allowed to make major
   policy statements, sanction projects, lay foundation stones
   and announce other measures to tempt the electorate
   after elections have been notified.

3. The Election Commission should be a multi-member body
   manned by persons of indubitable integrity, such as judges
   of the Supreme Court and the High Courts. They should
   be selected by a Board consisting of the Chief Justice of
   the Supreme Court, the Prime Minister and the leader of
   the opposition (or a representative of the opposition
   acceptable to all the groups).

4. Political parties must be required to submit election
   expense returns. Expenses incurred by parties on individual candidates including the general party programme
   should be included in the returns filed by candidates.

5. Use of radio, TV, government vehicles, aircraft and other government apparatus for party purposes should be forbidden to the ruling party except on terms of parity with opposition parties.
6. The age of voting must be reduced to 18 years.

In a Note for Discussion I had circulated on 11 November 1975 when there was some early kite-flying on the possibility of general elections in March 1976, I had commented that:

The government has replied to these and to other demands on electoral reforms in such unambiguous terms since 26 June 1975 that even a proposal for discussion on these matters with the dictator's regime would be an exhibition of mental imbalance on the part of the opposition.

I do not have to state that the situation, if anything, has deteriorated further and continues to deteriorate despite the recent moves of the dictator to release a few people. Mrs Gandhi has not only consolidated her own grip over the state machine, but she has quite successfully projected her son as the "only hope" for the country after her.

So, what do we do in the circumstances? Do we still prepare ourselves (though to me in the present situation even the very idea sounds pathetic) to take part in Mrs Gandhi's gigantic fraud on the Indian people and her gross abuse of all democratic ideals and norms?

Do we still fight the elections, and after the inevitable disaster once again repeat the same charges that have been made for twenty-five years?

Fighting elections under the existing conditions means giving respectability, credibility and legality to the existing electoral system. In the circumstances all subsequent wailing over the unequal conditions becomes demonstration in naivete. It neither impresses those who have further entrenched themselves in power, nor convinces the faithful who, after all, till the other day had been led to believe that they could achieve the impossible.

It is, therefore, necessary to clinch the issue now. Either the elections are fought after the agreed electoral reforms are introduced and after a reasonable time for "recovery", or the oppposition parties should boycott the elections.

It is said that boycott would result in our not having even a weak voice in Parliament. It is also said, foolishly, that the people given an opportunity would rally to our support and we can put in a good showing provided the legal, formal impediments such as the Emergency and Press censorship are removed. It is further said, and this appears to be the most telling argument, that boycott will not deter Mrs Gandhi from going ahead with the elections and that she will succeed in either weaning away dissidents or in actually creating new "opposition" parties who would contest the elections and that she would further make it possble for a pliant "opposition" to enter Parliament.

I believe that these arguments and objections stem from refusal to accept that Mrs Gandhi is a dictator who even if she should go through the farce of an election will never voluntarily surrender power. Nor will she hold an election if she were to be denied full participation by the oppposition; in any case her claim to legitimacy would be questionable if there were a boycott. Besides, we must profit by the experience of several past elections, and more particulary those after 1967 when Mrs Gandhi was installed as Prime Minister. In 1971, one important opposition leader produced a major thesis on how the 1971 general elections had been rigged. In West Bengal, the CPI (M) has been boycotting the State Assembly for the last five years on the gound that the elections to the State Assembly in 1972 were completely rigged. The Barpeta Lok Sabha by-election was a classic case of rigging; Madhubani in Bihar was another. Today, the stakes for Mrs Gandhi are bigger than ever before. If she holds elections, she will hold them for reasons that will ensure an overwhelming majority for her. She will also see to it that none of those who are likely to be troublesome is elected. The question is: Will the opposition oblige her by taking shelter behind some naive and foolish arguments?

The Socialist Party must take a definite stand on this issue. Our position should be that we shall participate in elections only if the rules under which they are to be held are framed to the satisfaction of the entire opposition and after the minimum period necessary to reorganise members and for the people and the Press to shed their fear has elapsed. What those rules are have been spelt out earlier in this Note. I want the National Committee not to prevaricate on this matter. On what we now decide to do will depend the future course of the struggle to restore democracy and to herald socialism in India. We should also persuade other parties to join with us in the boycott of the poll. If others do not agree to go along with us, that should not deter us from our determination.

A fair question that may be asked is: Are we to go it alone in this boycott and go into wilderness? I want the party to realise that unswerving determination and courage to fight the dictatorship is not to choose wilderness., On the contrary, the party will emerge after the uncompromising exhibition of determination and courage as a party deserving of the confidence of the people. In the meanwhile it will become the beacon light for the thousands of our youth and intellectuals who have started to bestir themselves. Adherence to principles, uncompromising determination and indomitable courage are qualities that we must practise and by example imbibe in our people. I suggest that we need not forsake principle and conviction for the sake of company.

I would ask the members of the National Committee to ponder over the points that I have raised and to appreciate that this is perhaps the most critical issue that the party has faced and the times are also the most critical for the country. If we falter and fail, neither the country nor history will forgive us. I would want the National Committee to give a call to the opposition to boycott the threatened elections unless the conditions for their being free and fair are assured and they are held only nine months to a year after "normalcy" is restored.

If all or some parties are not willing to join us in the boycott. then we must go it alone, if necessary. A holiday from parliamentary activity may actually do the party a great deal of good,

Sd/-
George Fernandes

APPENDIX C

Mr George Fernande's letter from prison to the General Secretary of the Socialist Party Mr Surendra Mohan

19 January 1977.

Dear Surendra,

Mrs Gandhi has dissolved the Lok Sabha and called for a fresh poll. It is obvious that she wants to have it on her own terms. The Emergency continues, civil liberties remain suppressed, the Press stays muzzled, the radio, TV, cinema and other media are used to sing glories of Mother and Son, the sword of MISA continues to hang over the heads of all political workers who may dare criticise her and—as today—activists of political parties continue to rot in jail.

In a note I had sent for consideration by the National Committee of the party earlier in the week, I had stated in detail the conditions under which the opposition could participate in the elections. In the event of the conditions not being fulfilled, I had pleaded for the boycott of the elections by the party and urged that other parties be also approached to join the boycott.

In announcing her decision to hold fresh elections in March, Mrs Gandhi has once again demonstrated her utter contempt for the opposition parties and particularly for those who were seeking a dialogue with her to restore normalcy. Evidently, she believes that whenever she calls the tune and whatever the tune she calls, the opposition will dance to it.

As I have argued in the note to the National Committee, it will be utterly suicidal for the opposition parties to oblige Mrs Gandhi by participating in the kind of elections she plans to have. There is only one course open to us and that is to boycott the poll. The National Committee must take a firm decision on boycotting the sham elections and deny Mrs Gandhi the legitimacy she is trying to secure through illegitimate means.

At the same time the party must give a call to all the big and small parties of the opposition—whatever their ideological hue—to make common cause to boycott the elections. While we may do our utmost to persuade them to boycott the poll, their reluctance or refusal should not in any way affect our stand on the boycott. Nor should a few gestures towards 'normalisation', such as release of most political prisoners, revocation of Emergency, which she is bound to make, influence our decision.

During his talks with Madhu Dandavate in Patna on January 8 and 9, JP had made it clear that he "is keen that the unified party should be an instrument to fight for civil liberties and for revocation of Emergency." He also wanted "the new party to be launched with this struggle perspective." I have repeatedly stated that I stand for unity for struggle. But if the new party should participate in the kind of elections that are now sought to be held, such a party by no stretch of imagination can be a party of struggle against dictatorship.

In the circumstances, we must insist on every party of the opposition taking a clear and unequivocal stand against Mrs Gandhi's bogus elections before we agree to merge into one party with them. This will be in keeping with JP's own perspective of unity and struggle. Such a stand should not be left for consideration and decision by the new party. The commitment by the constituent parties should be before the merger. If all other parties unfortunately choose to go their own way, then the only course open to us is to go it alone with the boycott and with the struggle. I know our weaknesses, but in times like these, it will not be the numbers that will ultimately count but the courage and character of those who refuse to bow to the wishes of a dictatorship.

I should like you to place this letter also for the consideration of the National Committee.

Greetings,

Yours sincerely,
Sd/
George Fernandes.

Statement released by Mr Jagjivan Ram in Press conference on 2 February 1977

We have supported Mrs Gandhi so far since 1969 because she had proclaimed a policy which promised to be the continuation of the best tradition of the Indian National Congress as adumbrated by Gandhiji. We extended to her our unstinted loyatly and support so far because she had promised to eliminate narrow personal loyalties and bossism from the Congress organisation, had announced various progressive measures and had given the assurance of ending social disparities and uplifting the scheduled castes, scheduled tribes and the weaker sections by ending poverty as conveyed by her slogan of "Garibi Hatao."

However, developments since the declaration of Emergency in June 1975 have generated the most ominous trends in our country, which seem to be reversing not merely the promises and professions of the Indian National Congress since 1969, but decency and integrity in public life and also the rudimentary norms of democracy. The internal democracy of the Congress organisation at all levels has been not only abridged but has almost been abolished. Indiscipline within the Congress both in organisational and parliamentary (legislative) wings has been not only tolerated but instigated and encouraged from above. The most dangerous procedures have been adopted to topple those Chief Ministers who do not submit to the dictates of some individuals though they enjoy comfortable majorities in their respective legislature parties. Such ousters are achieved through intrigue, threat and allurement unknown in the history of the Congress. In this way a system of concentrating power in a coterie or even an individual has been ruthlessly taken recourse to. The tendencies towards despotic rule in the Congress organisation as also in the administration of the country are increasing alarmingly. The basic tenets of democracy and socialism to which the Congress has been committed since the thirties are being violated with impunity. The device of authorisation has been invented to complete the process of authoritarianism. Congressmen at all levels do not like these trends but have been overawed into silence and are living in a suffocating condition. A silent majority in the Congress is restive and impatiently waiting for a lead to resurrect democracy in the organisation and in the country. Millions of Congressmen, students, youths, peasants and workers, intellectuals and masses gladly underwent untold suffering and sacrifice at the call of the motherland to free her from foreign subjugation. The motherland calls once again to guard and preserve democracy, to protect human values so that INDIA AND INDIA alone becomes strong and prosperous. It is in this context that we have taken the fateful decision to appeal directly to Congressmen, to youth, to intelligentsia and to the people in general to come forward and prevent the impending reversal of the basic directions of Indian political life set out before us by the founding fathers of the Republic. We are convinced that we would be open to the charge of gross dereliction of our duty and obligation to the people of our country if we did not take them into confidence at this decisive hour. Any suffering for the sake of the cause will not be shirked. We have faith in the people. We have chosen this moment to appeal to them in view of the fact that the coming general elections to the Lok Sabha provide perhaps the last opportunity for preventing the total reversal of the nation's cherished policies, and for correcting the illegitimacy that predominates in several aspects of our national life. We are, however, convinced that conditions are yet to be created for a free expression of the popular will and as such we demand in unequivocal terms:

—the immediate withdrawal of the Emergency;

—the repeal of MISA;

—the release of all political prisoners held under arbitrary laws;

—the repeal of the Prevention of Publication of Objectionable Matters Act;

—the restoration of the Feroze Gandhi Act ensuring immunity for the publication of parliamentary proceedings;

— the declaration by the Government that the police and para military forces shall not be used in the election in any manner that may intimidate the voters;

—the Government machinery shall not be used in any manner for the purpose of promoting the interest and image of any person in political life; and

—the Government's mass media, particularly the Radio and the Television, shall observe the norms that prevailed before Emergency.

Any party believing in parliamentary system of government cannot possibly consider going to the electorate to seek legitimacy for itself without fulfilling these minimum conditions for a free expression of the popular verdict.

We appeal to all right-thinking Congressmen, who cherish the democratic traditions of the Congress organisation, to seriously consider the grave impairment of democratic norms and procedures which has recently afflicated the Congress organisation. Many duly elected Congress committees at Pradesh and District levels have been arbitrarily replaced by ad hoc committees. The AICC, which has always been a predominantly elected body having only 10% nominated members with no voting rights, has of late, been reduced to a submissive ratifying committee with nearly half of its members selected by nomination. Political and organisational decisions of grave consequences have been announced at random by persons having no locus standi in the Congress organisation and such decisions have often been taken behind the back of even the Congress Working Committee. Therefore, now is the time for all Congressmen to assert themselves openly, and with the aid of the people, who hold the Indian Congress as the repository of their emergence to nationhood, to reverse the current drift to disaster.

We appeal to all right-thinking Congressmen, who have the interest of India's toiling millions in their heart to realise that the 20-point programme has virtually been pushed to the background, thanks to the emphasis on certain new programmatic points, and through a whole series of major concessions granted to vested interests, while denying the working class their rightful claims. In this connection, it is necessary to visualise the grave consequences of the manner in which land reforms have been relegated to a secondary position and the way the rule of law for all practical purposes has yielded place to rule of of men. This has seriously eroded the credibility of the highest authorities of the land on the one hand and has created grave feelings of insecurity in the minds of the poor masses as well as the minority communities on the other. The very purpose of all our social and economic programme is being defeated and the common people are being alienated from the Congress and the Government.

We are convinced that a leadership which alienates the minorities and the have-nots from the Congress organisation is throwing to the winds the most important plank of Indian National Congress and the Indian political system. We have chosen to come out openly at this hour also because we feel that such grave impairment of the confidence of the minorities may ultimately disrupt the integrity of the nation itself. We shall do all in our power to restore the confidence of the minorities and the weaker section of the people.

We would like to reiterate that our objective is the defence of the best tradition of the Indian National Congress, the restoration of decency and integrity in public life, and the prevention of the current drift of our democratic system in the direction of an authoritarian regime and self-centred establishment. We have decided to stand by the long-suffering people of this country, the poor and the deprived, no matter what price we have to pay.

In this solemn endeavour we seek the active co-operation of

all forward-looking forces of our country and we appeal to all
right-thinking Congressmen to respond to the call of their
conscience. This is a crucial moment when the defence
of democracy is the supreme task facing our nation. We go
into this crusade with unflinching faith in our people and the
triumph of our cause.

Index